Dee ~~" ... "~~

Love, Dad

THE BATTLES AT PLATTSBURGH

THE BATTLES AT
PLATTSBURGH

SEPTEMBER 11, 1814

KEITH A. HERKALO

FOREWORD BY DONALD E. GRAVES

Charleston · London

THE
History
PRESS

Published by The History Press
Charleston, SC 29403
www.historypress.net

The front cover image is known as "Macdonough's Victory." After 1815, many versions of the same arrangement were produced by artists, engravers and printers for use in historic texts and in adorning commemorative plates, bowls, vases and such over the years. For example, four versions were produced by Louis Garneray of France in the mid-1800s and are owned by the Wintertur Museum in Delaware. The earliest "claim" to having produced the arrangement was made by artist Hugh Reinagle, who, with engraver Benjamin Tanner, distributed prints in 1816; the "Tanner Print," as it is known, is the most widely known and distributed.

The unsung hero in the image story is a gentleman named Luther Stevens, a copper-plate engraver who happened to be at Plattsburgh during the naval battle. He sketched the scene as he watched it, presenting his preliminary sketch to Macdonough for his review of authenticity. In the fall of 1814, Stevens solicited subscription orders by advertisement in the local Plattsburgh paper. He returned to his home in Boston, produced the copper plate (larger than he advertised to his subscribers), printed the images and returned to Plattsburgh in the early spring of 1815, delivering prints of the work "Macdonough's Victory" to his subscribers—a year before Reinagle is said to have visited the region.

I continue to search for a surviving original Stevens print of the battle scene. Stevens returned to Boston, where he was known as an engraver and publisher of some renown. He died in 1858 at Mont Vernon, New Hampshire.

New York artist John J. Purdy's Culver Hill: September 6, 1814 appears on the rear cover.

First published 2012

Manufactured in the United States

ISBN 978.1.60949.516.9

Library of Congress CIP data applied for.

Contents

Foreword

It gives me a great deal of pleasure to contribute a foreword to Keith Herkalo's *The Battles at Plattsburgh: September 11, 1814.* I read the preliminary edition of the book with great interest, and I am glad that, in light of the forthcoming bicentennial of the War of 1812, Keith has decided to bring out this revised and upgraded version.

In my opinion, no other major battle of the War of 1812 has been as overlooked or as obscured as the 1814 battle of Plattsburgh. As Keith explains in his introduction, and as is evident throughout his text, this was the major British offensive of the war. That offensive did not, as many Americans think, take place in the Chesapeake operations of the summer, which saw the capture of Washington, the Battle of North Point and the bombardment of Fort McHenry. Dramatic as these events were, British senior leaders intended the 1814 campaign in the Chesapeake as a large raid to draw off American troops from the northern theatre of war.

And there should be no mistake that the northern theatre, which stretched along the international border from Lake Champlain to the Detroit River, was the cockpit of the War of 1812. Nearly 65 percent of the American regular army fought in this area from 1812 to 1815, and when Britain was able to send reinforcements to North America after the defeat of Napoleon, most went to Canada, not to points farther south. The heaviest fighting and the worst casualties of the war occurred in the north, and not in the Chesapeake or Louisiana. To most Americans, however, if the War of 1812 means anything, it conjures up images of the burning of the White House, the rockets' red glare over Fort McHenry, the frigate *Old Ironsides* and Andy Jackson and his band of buckskin-clad riflemen slaughtering Britons by the score at New Orleans while Johnny Horton sings in the background. Even as we approach the bicentennial, nothing much has changed; a few days ago, the United States Mint announced that it would issue two special coins in 2012—one would commemorate the bombardment of Fort McHenry and the other, the Battle of Baltimore.

Even if many Americans are unaware of the importance of the Battle of Plattsburgh, the citizens of that town in upstate New York are determined to preserve the memory of that important event in their history. Over the years, I have visited Plattsburgh a number of times during the annual commemorations in September, as either a tourist or an invited speaker. When I do, I have not only enjoyed myself tremendously, but I have also been impressed by the enthusiasm the people of Plattsburgh demonstrate and the respect they show for the past. For many years, Keith Herkalo has been involved in organizing these commemorations, and his interest increased to the point where he decided to write a book about what might well be called "America's Forgotten Victory." *The Battles at Plattsburgh* is the result.

The study of history is basically a process of accretion. One historian takes a subject so far; another historian then picks up the subject and extends it with new research. Keith Herkalo has wisely chosen to complement and expand the work of Allan S. Everest whose 1981 title, *The War of 1812 in the Champlain Valley*, was a major milestone in the historiography of the war, which is only too often cloaked in national chauvinism and myth. I still recall how impressed I was when I first read Everest because he had done impressive research *on both sides of the border*, maintained an objectivity untainted by nationalism and wrote clear and economical prose without wasting a word. When I first began writing seriously about the War of 1812, Everest was one of my models, and I think that if he were still with us, he would be very pleased with the book that follows.

Donald E. Graves
Maple Cottage
Valley of the Mississippi
Upper Canada

Acknowledgements

To my wife, Joy Demarse, I owe the greatest thanks. During my years of accompanying her to Montreal while she earned her doctorate at McGill University, I schlepped off to the McLennan Library to occupy my wait (for her classes to end) with research in the incredible 1812 collections. She urged that I sleep when she discovered me still typing or reading in the wee hours of many mornings and to press on as time permitted. Her patience, encouragement, proofreading and advice fostered my completion of this work. As a teacher of English, she shuddered at my first draft and the self-published, limited edition—somewhat scrubbed, my individuality remains in this final form.

To Dr. Allan Everest, now deceased, for encouraging my quest for the truth and a deliberate, systematic search for primary-source data. I'd hope that if he were here today, he'd nod "well done."

To Donald E. Graves for his encouragement, advice and the kind offer to write the foreword to this work.

To the myriad historians, societies, libraries and museums in the United States and Canada, too numerous to mention by name, for their contributions in pointing me to resources. I owe a special thanks to the Special Collections staffs at Plattsburgh State University's Feinberg Library, St. Lawrence University's Owen D. Young Library and the University of Michigan's Clements Library and to the staff of the Department of the Navy's Naval Historical Center and the U.S. Naval Academy's Nimitz Library.

To archaeologist Dr. Timothy Abel, for sharing my faith in the work of Dr. Everest and joining my crusade to identify the location of the 1812 winter encampment site of the U.S. Fifteenth Regiment, Pike's Cantonment.

Flags. *Author's sketch.*

To my good friend Gordie Little and my colleagues in the history community of Plattsburgh for listening to my historical rants and theories—always providing solid advice and a ground for me to land on, what really happened versus what's been said.

To my sister, Elyse Zielinski, for her graphic art talents and for producing the cover art and illustrations in the last moments of readying this work.

To the City of Plattsburgh for its gracious permission to reproduce portions of the City's Heritage Trail illustrations.

To Dean Mosher, John J. Purdy and the Battle of Plattsburgh Association for their collective permission to reproduce images of their artistic works.

To Whitney Tarella and the staff of The History Press for their guidance and support in publishing this work.

To you, the reader, for your interest in the battles at Plattsburgh, the most important battles of the War of 1812. Churchill and Roosevelt recognized the incredible events at Plattsburgh. Bathurst provided us with the roadmap.

Introduction

M y intents in this humble work are several:

First, to complete, in so far as is possible, the work of Dr. Allan S. Everest as it relates to the battles at Plattsburgh. In an interview with Dr. Everest shortly before his death in 1997, I had the pleasure to discuss some of my theories and research. Dr. Everest's *The War of 1812 in the Champlain Valley* is referenced among serious historians as the standard regarding Plattsburgh's place in the War of 1812. Recent events in which I have had a hand (the positive identifications of the sites of Pike's Cantonment and the burials on Crab Island), and the location of what I believe are overlooked and/or little-referenced primary documents, shed new light on the work of this noted historian and complete some of his long-sought quests.[1]

Second, to bring to consciousness the size and scope of the Plattsburgh-area battlefield events made evident by the archaeological certainties now available. While the naval engagement on Cumberland Bay seems to be treated more often and more dramatically, the task and accomplishments of General Macomb and his regular/militia forces are somehow shortchanged. (On September 11, 1814, he commanded more militia forces than regular.) The naval battle arena of Cumberland Bay encompasses some ten thousand acres; the land events spread over twenty thousand acres. National Battlefield designation is being sought for the combination thirty thousand acres.

Third, to address numerous errors and unsubstantiated "facts" that have made their way into contemporary works regarding the subject. My aim is to present the events leading up to the battles at Plattsburgh with accuracy and a minimum of assumption.

Fourth, the War of 1812 has sometimes been treated as unimportant and forgotten. The farther removed in time from an event, the less the consciousness. I believe that if we approach the subject in the context of its importance at the time, we can begin to understand its impact on our then-young nation and its significance in our history.

The History Channel's 2006 offering *The First Invasion* went a long way to address the gap in national visibility of the War of 1812. The docudrama did cover the attacks on Washington and Baltimore by a British force of approximately 4,500 and the fateful attack on New Orleans. It is widely known, however, that these attacks were only diversions executed at the prince regent's direction. The well-documented June 1814 "secret order" from Bathurst, Britain's secretary of war (made public shortly after the Treaty of Ghent) is a key document that exposes British planning for the end of the war. Plattsburgh, the focus of the British plan as ordered by Secretary of War Bathurst, was to see the war's largest concentration of British troops. Just across the border north of Plattsburgh, some 14,000 British troops were gathered for the invasion of the United States. While individual battles and skirmishes were covered, the British plan of diverting American attention away from the Lake Champlain region to attack Plattsburgh, the single-most strategically crafted event of the British war plan (feint at Sackets Harbor, attacks on the eastern coastal villages, the "invasion" of Baltimore, the attack on New Orleans, etc.) was not covered in the History Channel presentation or in the 2011 PBS television presentation *The War of 1812*. Often overlooked by scholars, Bathurst's plan, the gist of which was first proposed by Sir John Borlase Warren, commander in chief of the North American Station, in letters (in November 1812 and February 1813) to Viscount Melville, First Lord of the Admiralty, is perhaps the most significant and interesting facet of the war. Imagine the result if the British had succeeded at Plattsburgh![2]

And fifth, to present some rather curious items that I've happened upon in the course of discovery: the fun "stuff" that has entertained my senses of curiosity and intrigue. For the months and years leading up to the battles at Plattsburgh, I have chosen to use as my point of reference the journal entries of Eleazer Williams. He chronicled the War of 1812 from in and around the village of Plattsburgh and the North Country. His journal entries span the entire period from 1812 to 1815 and form the framework on which those years leading up to the battles are anchored (the battles being stories themselves).

Williams, the Caughnawaga-born Native American unfortunately confused by Charles Muller with the Williams from Bakersfield, Vermont,[3] was a colorful personality, a Puritan Congregational minister who would eventually convert to Episcopalian. He was prone to aggrandizement and self-promotion, as some have pointed out, and yet, the majority of the wartime events detailed by Williams have been spoken of by respectable others: corroboration for his observations of the times and circumstances as seen through the eyes of a deeply religious "Indian." His is the only known firsthand chronicle of Plattsburgh's and the North Country's involvement in the War of 1812.

The subtitle was chosen not to take away from the tragic destruction of New York City's World Trade Center towers, which occurred on September 11, 2001, but to note the significance of the date that both events share. Both were invasions on our soil.

1

Unsettled Times (Pre-1812)

The town that was established as Plattsburgh experienced significant growth in its first twenty years. The settlement initiated by Zephaniah Platt and others who received land patents from Governor George Clinton after the Revolution (1787) flowered in the years after the conflict. The patents specified that Platt establish a viable community within seven years from the date of issue; if Platt was successful, the lands would transfer to a grant.

Location, location, location is what we hear in regard to business. Lake Champlain was the roadway of transportation during this period; Plattsburgh was a crossroad. There was what we today would call a mass-marketing effort directed at those with adventurous spirits and entrepreneurial natures. Farmers, crafters, those with business acumen and those who provided services to the whole (ministers, doctors, teachers and the like) were lured by incentives and opportunity and relocated to the North Country.

The community grew steadily through the years. By the early 1800s, Plattsburgh had become an important stop for commerce up and down the lake corridor. Hostile feelings toward the British grew, as well, the result of recent British actions and the simmering memory of the War for Independence. Brackenridge noted that Great Britain's interdiction of all intercourse with France "operated exclusively on the United States, who were the only remaining neutrals." U.S. trade abroad was disrupted.

In the late spring of 1807, British frigates were stationed off the coast of Virginia when Master Commandant Charles Gordon, acting captain of the U.S. ship *Chesapeake*, weighed anchor and set course for the Mediterranean. The British vessel *Leopard* overtook the *Chesapeake* and fired on it. Gordon's

Above: "The Chesapeake and Leopard."
From The Military Heroes of the War
of 1812.

Left: "The Impressment of an American
Seaman." *From* Sea Power in Its
Relations to the War of 1812.

crew and vessel were not prepared for engagement in reality or spirit; they were quickly disabled and boarded by the British crew. Four of the U.S. crew were identified as British deserters and removed from the vessel. With sixteen wounded and three dead, the damaged *Chesapeake* repaired to Hampton Roads, and news quickly spread. Thomas Jefferson issued a proclamation in early July that expelled British warships from American waters.

In 1809, in answer to the threat of war and the defiant and open trade with Canada, it was felt that there was a need to establish a naval fleet on Lake Champlain to enforce the established embargo. In the spring of that year, two gunboats were built for Lake Champlain, and a young midshipman, James Cooper, with just one year of naval service, found himself assigned to duty on the lake. Cooper served through the summer, leaving in November of that year after being assigned to the *Wasp* on the eastern coast. Cooper's father died in the winter of 1809, leaving to the young officer his comfortable estate. Cooper remained in the naval service into the spring of 1811, when, after marrying, he resigned his commission. With the inheritance of his father's estate ensuring a comfortable living, the young Cooper began to write stories steeped in the knowledge of firsthand naval and frontier experiences. In 1826, after successfully petitioning the New York legislature, an act was approved that changed his last name to Fenimore Cooper, in honor of his mother's family. Fenimore Cooper went on to publish many frontier adventure and naval works.[1]

The municipality named the "Village of Plattsburgh" was not legally formed until 1815; but by 1811, the thriving business center, the center of population and the center of service and entertainment at the mouth of the Saranac River became known as "the village." (For a more complete discussion of the early history and growth of the area, see Peter Palmer's *History of Lake Champlain* and Allan Everest's *The War of 1812 in the Champlain Valley*.)

While we're at this point, I'd like to address the subject of the so-called controversy regarding the spelling of the name of Plattsburgh the municipality. Some say that the spelling should be "Plattsburg," without the "h." Norman Ansley, in presenting an otherwise interesting collection of names and facts, states:

> *In 1814, the City of Plattsburg* [sic] *spelled its name without an* h *ending. This was confirmed by an employee of the Plattsburg City Hall who said original documents from the War are without the* h...*The additional* h *has never been recognized by the Post office.*

"Sir George Prevost." *From* How Canada Was Held for the Empire.

Contrary to some local stories, and the statements of Mr. Ansley, the spelling of the name of the municipality that was/is Plattsburgh has never changed (see Appendix I).

The village was part of what was then the District of Champlain, which reported large quantities of exports from the area in 1811: pork, cider, corn, butter, lard, candles, leather, potash, soap, tea, tobacco, tallow, boots, shoes, lumber in pine and oak, wooden boat spars (masts, yards from which sails are hung, etc.), cask and barrel staves, ash oars and walnut handspikes (wooden levers).[2]

The year 1811 saw the arrival of Sir George Prevost at Quebec. He had been sent to deal with the divisive and hostile factions of English and Canadian patriots, a situation that Sir James Craig, his predecessor, had not been able to resolve. Prevost's task was to work to bring the two parties together, creating an atmosphere that would be necessary in dealing with the Americans to the south.

Through the summer and the fall of that year, tensions between the United States and Britain raised calls for war from the Congress of Madison's government. The disruption of trade, the capture of American ships and the impressments of U.S. seamen stirred angry sentiment. The British army had amassed forty thousand troops in Portugal and was surrounding *Ciudad Rodrigo*, trapping the French troops within it and stranding U.S. goods in the markets of Lisbon.[3]

There was virtually no standing army or navy to defend the United States, let alone take any offensive actions. A looming unrest fermented along the northern U.S. border. The growing U.S. population pushed north and west into the territory known as Indiana, hunting lands controlled by the tribal chiefs Tecumseh and Pontiac. The continuing struggle led to confrontation between Tecumseh's warriors and such U.S. forces as could be mustered from militia and the Fourth U.S. Regiment at Tippecanoe. Tecumseh sought the aid of the British in securing his territory against the encroaching U.S. population. The new Governor General Prevost instructed Major General Sir Isaac Brock to "find a clear but delicate way of letting the Indians know that in case of war, we expect aid of 'our brothers.'"[4]

The alliance between the Native Americans and the British fanned the flames of congressional fury. Madison delivered a message to Congress on November 5 explaining the state of affairs in Europe, the presence of British war ships "hovering on our coasts" and the need to increase the security of the country. He called for an increase in the regular force, an auxiliary force, volunteers and militia and an "enlargement" of the manufacture of cannons, small arms and munitions.[5]

Madison's call extended to the navy, which, in its November report to Congress, indicated that the entire gunboat fleet of the United States consisted of only sixty-five commissioned vessels, with seven others under repair and sixty-two in "ordinary" ("pickled," as we say today). Britain had hundreds of ships. Skeen states that "Congress at Jefferson's urging increased the size of the regular force to approximately 10,000, although the actual level never exceeded 6,000 before 1812."[6]

The non-importation law was openly challenged by smugglers; the revenue collectors were thwarted in their efforts to enforce the law. In the North Country, Lake Champlain, the major avenue of transportation and commerce to and from Canada, was not patrolled—a serious breach of the security that Madison sought. The navy would be called upon to play a more active role in the country's enforcement actions.

"A Naval Engagement in 1812–14." *From* How Canada Was Held for the Empire.

On November 29, Representative Peter B. Porter of the House Committee on Foreign Relations reported:

> *The United States as a sovereign and independent power, claim the right to use the ocean, which is the common and acknowledged highway of nations, for the purposes of transporting, in their own vessels, the products of their own soil and the acquisitions of their own industry, to a market in the ports of friendly nations, and to bring home, in return, such articles as their necessities or convenience may require—always regarding the rights of belligerents, as defined by the established laws of nations. Great Britain, in defiance of this incontestable right, captures every American vessel bound to or returning from a port where her commerce is not favored; enslaves our seamen, and in spite of our remonstrances perseveres in these aggressions. To wrongs so daring in character, and so disgraceful in their execution, it is impossible that the people of the U. States should remain indifferent. We must now tamely and quietly submit, or we must resist by those means which God has placed within our reach.*

Everest noted that the North Country "communities enjoyed important trade connections with Canada which they did not want to see disrupted, but more urgently they realized that if war came it would strike them first."[7]

On December 27 in Plattsburgh, militia major Thomas Miller called for his regiment to rendezvous at the Union Coffeehouse on January 7.[8] Congress weighed in on the increasing issue. Representative Porter of New York sought support for but failed in an effort to raise a "20,000 man provisional army of short-term volunteers." The shortfall in manning was reintroduced when David R. Williams, chair of the House Committee on the Militia, sought the raising of an additional twenty thousand regular troops because "the militia was unreliable."[9] Williams's bill, introduced on December 29, was hotly debated into the spring and, after several amendments, would not see passage until the early part of 1813.

An unsteady course for war had been set both internationally and locally.

2
War Is Declared (1812)

Throughout the remainder of the winter of 1811 nothing of great military significance occurred in or about Plattsburgh. In Washington, Madison appointed the aging Boston customs broker Henry Dearborn as one of two major generals. By April, Dearborn, the de facto chief of staff "had developed the outline of a plan for the conquest of Canada. Its main thrust was to the north from Lake Champlain to Montreal although supporting campaigns were to be launched from Sackets Harbor, Niagara, and Detroit."[1]

Naval actions along Lake Champlain were to concentrate on the interdiction of contraband. The condition of the two poorly maintained U.S. vessels on Lake Champlain, the *Eagle* (commanded by Lieutenant Sidney Smith) and the *Growler* (commanded by Sailing Master James Loomis) were spoken of by Governor Tompkins in his letter to Naval Agent John Bullus of New York: "One of them partly sunk in the water and the seams of both of them so open as almost to admit the hand."[2]

As war approached, the vessels would be repaired to sail the lake between Plattsburgh and Burlington as local recruitment efforts and military activity grew. It was noted that Horace Bucklin Sawyer of Burlington was appointed as a midshipman and assigned to the *Eagle*[3] and Captain Reuben Sanford of Wilmington was chosen to command the Eighth Regiment of the detached militia.[4]

In the same month, Thomas Macdonough, eventually to be assigned to Lake Champlain, wrote from Middletown, Connecticut, to the secretary of the navy requesting that he be reinstated in the navy.[5] Across the northern border, Major General Brock met with the Iroquois to solicit

"Commodore Thomas Macdonough, USN."
From A Pictorial History of the New World.

their support in the British efforts but met with difficulty when he "suggested that the Iroquois form three companies of warriors and rotate one each month to the Niagara Peninsula to help guard the border." The Iroquois of New York would ultimately adopt a position of neutrality.

Congress declared a state of war on June 18. As evidenced by announcements in the local newspaper, local patriotic sentiments and military activity quickly swelled:

It is with lively satisfaction we give publicity to the following articles of association of the "Veteran Exempts" of this town. It is with pleasure we remark, that the glowing patriotism which it exhibits, is become almost general throughout this county and we hope throughout the country. In this association we test the spirit of the country—we recognize the true character of freemen, and learn how little a free country has to fear, when every breast, even of the aged and exempt, form a firm and glowing rampart to our nations honor and safety. In this patriotic offer of the exempts mostly Veterans of our Revolution, we see the same spirit which animated our countrymen in '76; which age cannot quench, which time could not diminish and which our recent injuries served only to awaken into action. Let our youth enkindle at it and endeavor to emulate them. The need of praise is also due to the back settlers of this town, who we understand have organized and officered a volunteer company which is already nearly full. It ought also to be noted, as honorable to this frontier county, that the requisitions which have yet been made by law, have almost universally been complied with by volunteers; and that the only company of Artillery in this county have volunteered under Capt. Joseph I. Green, and are now in requisition. This is as it should be; evincing themselves worthy to be free, and constantly anticipating the wishes of their country, in defence of her rights, they render compulsion or requisition unnecessary.

War Is Declared (1812)

The articles of association are as follows. "Every Citizen possessing a genuine spirit of Patriotism is called upon to be at his post. There are many of us, who by law are exempt from personal military service: but the love of country, the laws of honor, our wives, our children, our flocks and herds, and our very soil, from whose bosom we have hitherto drawn such rich abundance, call upon us for defence. Let then every unworthy principle be banished. While we pray for peace let us prepare for War. Let us rally round the standard of our Country and our Independence. Let us enrol [sic] ourselves among their defenders.

We whose names are hereunto subscribed, do hereby associate to form a company of volunteers, to be denominated the VETERAN EXEMPTS, for the defence of our own and the neighboring towns. As soon as fifty have enlisted they are to choose their own officers—apply for commissions and arms and to act as occasion may require, always giving a preference to the protection of the associates, and at other times to be subject to the requisitions of the military chief on the station.

To serve without pay, and expect nothing but our rations when on actual duty from home, and the approbation of our consciences and our country. Plattsburgh, June 29, 1812

Here follow the names of 142 of the citizens of this town, all of whom are exempt, by law, from doing military duty. Officers chosen by the Company.

Gen. Mel. L Woolsey, Captain.

Judge Kinner Newcomb, 1ˢᵗ Lieut.

Capt. John Stevenson, 2ᵈ Lieut

Col. Marinus F. Durand, Ensign.

The non-commissioned officers are of a similar age and standing in society with the above.

The 7ᵗʰ Regiment of detached militia of this State, commanded by Col James Green, arrived at head quarters (in this town) on the 12ᵗʰ instant. Two companies of this Regiment have marched to Champlain.

Col. Thomas Miller's Regiment, made up from the counties of Essex, Clinton & Franklin, has been called out and stationed at Champlain and Chateaugay.

The recruiting for the Army of the U. States, in this village, through the unremitting goal and activity of Lieut. David Curtis, has surpassed the most sanguine expectations. Between 30 and 40 active young men have been enlisted in this town.[6]

Even as local emotions grew more patriotic, many local sentiments were expressed by Peter Sailly, the local revenue agent, who wrote to the secretary of the treasury in July:

> *The British brig of war the* Prince Edward, *repairing at St. Johns. We have no forces on this lake, nor a battery. The gun boats are out of repair. I am informed by a friend at Washington that the invasion of Canada is not contemplated to take place very soon. We must therefore be here on the defensive. But the British have begun hostilities by taking our fort at Michillmackinac. They may continue where there is a prospect of success. I think the regular troops ought to be near the frontiers, instead of being placed at Albany. Our inhabitants are alarmed and are moving off. There is not a single stand of arms in Vermont, nor a single man ordered to the protection of our frontier.*[7]

Not to be disregarded in the war atmosphere that existed in the North Country was uncertainty regarding U.S. relations with the local Indian tribes. General Dearborn, seeking to calm relations with the Indians and intelligence concerning the strengths and movements of the enemy near the border sought a confidential source who could address both situations. He directed Major General Benjamin Mooers of the local militia to consult with Peter Sailly; all deliberation and correspondence regarding the selection of such a person were to be strictly secret.[8]

The person in whom they would place their trust was Caughnawaga-born Congregational minister Eleazer Williams. Williams, whose roots were within the Iroquois nation, started a journal of his wartime

Benjamin Mooers. *From the* Pictorial Field Book of the War of 1812.

"Eleazer Williams." *From* Harper's Encyclopedia of United States History.

efforts on July 27, 1812, beginning, "I am sent for to prevent the Indians from taking the hatchet against the Americans."[9]

As militia interests grew, the local Veteran Exempts (one of two known local exempt organizations, the other being the Silver Grays of Chesterfield), who had organized at the end of the previous month, received acceptance by the governor and were authorized brevet ranks in accordance with Section 35 of the 1809 New York Militia Law. An exempt group consisted of a company of forty-five or more volunteers "exempt by law from Military duty, on account of service in the late War, or age."[10] They designed as their standard a black flag reminiscent of a "Jolly Roger." It bore a skull, crossed bones, a rattlesnake and thirteen silver stars.[11]

General Dearborn continued discussions with Eleazer Williams into August and offered payment at the rate of $400 per year, with rations and travel expenses, "to afford you the means in the winter seasons for improving your Education."[12] Williams agreed and was issued papers informing General Mooers of the secret nature of his employment and directing support for Williams and his family.[13] In early August, Williams was the guest of General Dearborn at Greenbush; he recorded the event in his journal:

> *Was received in camp by the General and his aids, his military family, indeed, with a courtesy that was not only gratifying but highly flattering.*

While there, was entertained with great hospitality, and all the time in the midst of plumes, golden epaulets, silver spoons, and red sashes... This was the first step of my being entangled with the war party of the country. They wanted my services and all their maneuvers about me had been for this end. I saw with much regret that I had committed myself unknowingly and undersigned.[14]

From that point on, Williams would travel the North Country connecting with his all-Indian "Secret Corps of Observation." This woods-skilled Native American group traveled the North Country seemingly undetected and passed significant intelligence information to the officers of the United States. Indians were generally treated with disdain, but as Williams observed, his corps "obtained much information as to the condition of things at the north. The officers paid great attention to these Indians from policy."[15] Williams himself traveled with credentials given him by General Mooers.[16] At the end of August, he journeyed to Albany "and sat up all night with General Dearborn communicating intelligence and arranging plans for the future."

Dearborn had just been informed by letter from Mooers of troop strength and movement of British regulars north of the border and that the roadways near the border had been obstructed to prevent American movement north.

"Colonel Zebulon Pike." *From* How Canada Was Held for the Empire.

In the same letter, Mooers told General Dearborn of revenue agent Peter Sailly having "had a paralytic fit, very severe, which injured his speech considerably"; he added that Sailly "is getting the better of it."[17] After corroborating the information gathered by Mooers, Williams was sent south to meet with the newly appointed Northern Army General Bloomfield at Whitehall before proceeding to the north again.[18]

Bloomfield's new command at Plattsburgh consisted of approximately eight thousand regulars, volunteers and militia;[19] the primary units were the Sixth Regiment under Colonel Jonas Simonds and the Fifteenth Regiment under Colonel Zebulon

Pike.[20] Bloomfield's arrival coincided with the end of an Armistice arranged by General Dearborn and British Colonel Baynes[21] and a general buildup of the British and American naval activities on Lake Champlain.

Williams noted the gunboat salute that announced the arrival of Bloomfield on September 9 and detailed the initial briefing, at which he introduced the general to the status of Indian relations (having previously negotiated with the North Country's Indian chiefs at Chateaugay and French Mills, now named Fort Covington, seeking their cooperation in the cause of the United States). He gave specifics of the intelligence information that had been garnered by the Indian Rangers of the Secret Corps of Observation: "the force of the enemy, the state of his defenses, the movements of his troops, the strength of his navy, and the condition of the roads from Champlain to L'Acadia plains."[22]

In early September, the navy purchased five sloops (*Hunter*, *Champlain*, *Juno*, *Jupiter* and *Fox*)[23] and contracted for 160 bateaux, each "37 feet long and 8 wide, and will carry 40 or 50 men. It is said contracts are made for building 60 in addition to the above number."[24] Concurrent with these actions, Lieutenant Thomas Macdonough arrived at Burlington.[25]

Bloomfield reported to the secretary of war the status of the ground forces, recent naval activities, personnel information and a recommendation for an

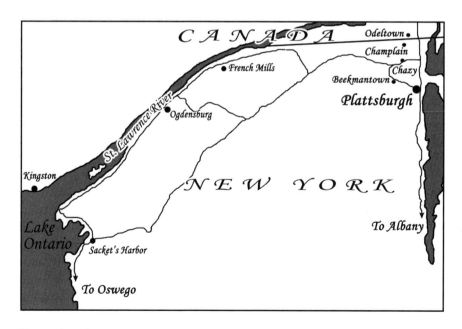

The northern front. *Adapted by Elyse Zielinski, 2012.*

appointment to fill an officer vacancy within Pike's Fifteenth Regiment.[26] He did the same, but in greater fashion, for General Dearborn, sending Major Bleeker with a map and intelligence information. Bleeker could address Bloomfield's concerns from firsthand knowledge, passing to Dearborn the dynamics of the frontier battlefield.

There were significant activities by a company of Voltiguers (light infantry) and Indians just north of the border, which alarmed the local population to the point of fleeing south and into Vermont. Bloomfield proposed that General Prevost had instructed the abatis of the countryside (obstruction of roadways with felled trees) and erection of a brush fence between the border and his troops (spread from St. Johns to La Prairie, the advance of the army being at Isle aux Noix). Bloomfield wrote:

> *The amount of the regulars has been greatly exaggerated. Some other travelers coming from Canada inform that there is not more than a militia company at St. Johns but that a [*"Regt of Nova Scotia" or "Royal Scotts"*] with less militia were in Saturday last at Isle aux Noix where the enemy are fortifying & the discipline very strict. The 41 & 49 Regts are in upper Canada.*
>
> *We must, my dear Genl, command the Lake—on hand there is no danger but from Indians that thirst for blood & scalps—Pickets & patrols from the Militia between the Lake and Saranac & from the Saranac west to the road. Cumberland neck & dear river posses by the 6,000 regular well manned. The [112] Regt are principally on fatigue in cutting away the young pine & turning the road from the Lake so as to clear & secure the encampment from surprise.*
>
> *Lt. Smith in addition to a 9-pounder mounted yesterday, a 3-pounder taken from the arsenal & has a detachment of 30 men & prevents the passage of all vessels above Cumberland head, without my passport—one only has been given to bring the Familys of persons sent out of Canada & collected on the great Chazy…I have the tenor to command, & which has inspired confidence in the inhabitants.*

He went on to report on the medical conditions that existed and, with the increase in troops, the need to establish a hospital at Plattsburgh. Dr. William Beaumont, attached to the Sixth Regiment, detailed the prevailing illnesses: "Typhus, Dysentaries and Rheumatism."[27]

Both sides had begun to focus on preparations for defense and the coming of winter. Bloomfield ordered that no vessel was to "sail to the Northward of Cumberland head—without a passport from the commanding officer."[28] Confident in his ability to defend the lake and the lines as established, he further ordered that the lake's only steamboat be chartered for military use and sail vessels be purchased and armed.[29] Bloomfield met with General Mooers, the local militia commander, from whom he requested suggestions regarding an appropriate place to establish a winter encampment for the army. In reporting to General Dearborn on his conversation with General Mooers, Bloomfield revealed his position relating to the regard in which he held the militia:

> *Respectful attention shall be paid to General Moers [sic]—but as I hold myself obedient only to yourself & accountable to my country. I shall not deem it my duty to be influenced or in the least directed by any Militia officer whatsoever.*[30]

The professional rift between regulars and militia would continue throughout the next several years (and, to some extent, exists today, hence the mildly derogatory terms "weekend warrior" and "gentleman soldier"). The unprofessional part-time militia remained a subject of discussion throughout the war. Militia forces were said to have behaved unprofessionally until tested at some length in training or battle; their worth would be proven in the coming Plattsburgh conflict.

The professional rift notwithstanding, it was militia General Mooers's response to Bloomfield's interest for a proper winter encampment location that resulted in Mooers's recommendation being accepted by Bloomfield: "Under all circumstances the most eligible place appears to me is on the south side of the River Saranac about two miles from this village. The timber generally pine and suitable size for hutting. There is likewise hard timber. The river [is] in front and difficult to cross as well in the winter as in the summer." This strategically important location, which had been surveyed the year before, would later become significant in each of the two coming years.[31]

Preparations for the winter continued at Plattsburgh and Burlington. Bloomfield ordered tents, kettles and other supplies to Burlington and two brass ten-pounders to be sent to Plattsburgh. He also ordered that blockhouses be built.[32]

Thus began what Everest termed the "Tragic First Winter." Everest's treatment of military life in Plattsburgh in the winter of 1812 is perhaps best appreciated when augmented with the observations of surgeons Mann and Beaumont.[33] To permit an adequate picture of the situation existing at Plattsburgh during this period, a few additional pieces of information need to be added.

Negotiations with and accommodations for the North Country Native Americans increased; subsistence payments, transportation and other perquisites were provided for them. Bloomfield acknowledged and reluctantly recognized the importance of the alliance with the Native American community, feared for its mannerisms but now courted for its talents.[34]

Late summer activity on the lake saw the sinking and raising of gunboat *#170* near Cumberland Head,[35] the grounding (later recovery) of the gunboat *Hunter*[36] and the contracting of the Vermont steamboat in the service of the United States.[37] Bloomfield placed a detachment from the Eleventh Infantry onto the sloop *Hunter* with orders to halt all lake traffic going north of Cumberland Head and to interdict any enemy vessel attempting to sail south.[38] He had found a creative way to deal with his personnel shortages and gain apparent control of the lake.

American army movements in the remainder of September and through much of the month of October appear to have been replacement activities, with troops being sent to Chazy, Champlain, Constable, Chateaugay and French Mills. Typical of the general's defensive direction was the following:

> *Two companies of at least fifty men each with as many officers and musik, to be detached by Brig. Genl Petit from the militia at this place—to march tomorrow* [September 24] *for Champlain under command of Major Lackorder, who will relieve Lieut. Col Miller in command on the location.*
>
> *One company of at least fifty men with arms, officers & musik to be detailed by Brig Genl Petit from the militia at this post—to proceed to Major Young's Quarters at Chateaugay.*[39]
>
> *Major Sheriden will proceed to the lines with the two companys detached agreeable to the orders of yesterday. Lt. Col. Miller is relieved in command & is permitted to return to P. Major Sheriden will not pass the lines or provoke aggression from the enemy but repel the enemy if attacked & protect the inhabitants & secure his quarters & accommodations of the troops under his command by erecting Block houses in defensible situations. Correct information of the force of the enemy to be forwarded by express to Head Quarters. No intercourse of the inhabitants with the Enemy to be permitted on any Pretense whatsoever.*[40]

War Is Declared (1812)

Bloomfield addressed shortages in maintaining the increasing troop strength:

> *You will observe with regret, how inadequate are the military stores in the arsenal, to supply the requisitions called for marked B. to move 100 men as ordered as by D.—as by configuring supply E. Captn. Lyons & Higbee's companies, the whole but 58 men, are under similar orders to assemble & reinforce Major Young at Chateagay & the French Mills. Bisdale's company of volunteers Riflemen consists of 24 men only. They encamp with the U.S. troops being regulars as will Enigh's company of cavalry when it shall have arrived. Genl. Petit having a cause for trial will move to Albany to where I refer your Excellency for information of the situation of this post & those of the actual wants of the militia & the necessity of knowing speedily as possible for them particularly in an ample supply of blankets, shoes, knapsacks, canteens, tin cups, spades, axes & two or 3 grindstones.*[41]

Relations with the North Country's Native Americans began to get more complicated. In one instance, Bloomfield ordered: "Paul Racoon a Cock or Indian will be furnished with six pounds of Pork a week to support himself… untill further orders."[42] In another, Bloomfield wrote:

> *Col Clark having requested permission to visit Albany will present himself at Head Quarters, with Eleazer Williams, Genl. Tall Man & his aid Col Vadruel, Indian Chief who will explain their mission & who may be carefully employed in Col. Clark's opinion. Tobel Benuhois, a warrior who came with the Indians & has returned. I have advanced $30 hard Dollars—3 kegs of Powder & 400 musket balls. Col. Clarke gave him a rifle & powder horn Genl Tallman has been presented with a sword by me—Vadruel, a sword by Col. Clark. E. Williams will explain their expectations—by what I learn they will expect to be dressed like army officers of their rank in complete uniform with epaulets, coced hat, &c. In a former communication I mentioned I had advanced E.W.'s $50 & to Capt Jacob Francis & the 2 Ind's with him $10 each so that with the sword presented to Genl. Tallman I have expenses which, with $10 to a Frenchman who lives near the lines, I advanced by the orders of Mr. Sailly—making in the whole $150.*[43]

Eleazer Williams had begun to make himself quite useful in the American efforts by arranging meetings with key members of the Indian community. These contacts would be important in the coming months in recruiting members for Williams's organization, the "Secret Corps of Observation," the skillful intelligence-gathering Indian scouts. The complicated relationships among Governor Tompkins, Dearborn, Bloomfield and Williams had their beginnings in the acknowledgement of a need and the recognition of the provider's status through titles, uniforms, money and supplies given to ease the lives of certain tribal families—i.e., politics.

Bloomfield, after personally proposing locations at Point Au Roche and Chazy, grudgingly agreed with General Mooers's suggested winter cantonment location on the sand hill south of the Saranac River, some miles outside the village. He sent Colonel Clark to Albany with requisitions for materials necessary "in making huts for 4 regts as ordered and calculated by Cols. Pike, Lardner & Clark." Ironically, the delivery of the requested materials was to be made "to Lieut. Mooers of the 23rd Regt., son of Genl. Mooers."

Bloomfield, mindful of activities north of the border, reported a buildup of British forces at Isle aux Noix and elsewhere and their movement from camps to winter quarters. On October 10, he observed that snow was expected; two days later, there was snow. In the rain that followed, Bloomfield took note that, of the 1,200 men in his four-regiment charge at Plattsburgh, almost 25 percent were sick, and winter was just beginning.[44] Dr. James Mann described the early October weather as changing suddenly: "Very cold with early frosts."[45]

While increasing military activity took place in the Niagara area to the west, troop movements in the Plattsburgh area were minimal and defensive; considerable efforts were concentrated in building up resources. In addition to the two brass ten-pounders received from Burlington, the land artillery grew by one six-pounder, three four-pounders and two three-pound cannons. Bloomfield noted that meat and bread were plentiful but complained again of logistical problems. He reported the short supply of flint and musket ammunition, telling Dearborn, "We have not, nor cannot command as you will see by the returns transmitted, more than 12 cartridges per man." And they were running out of cartridge paper. The cartridge paper shortage continued throughout the month of October until the frustrated Bloomfield ordered that cartridges be fashioned from newspaper. The cutting of the trees for huts raised another logistical shortcoming: the supplied axes were made of such soft-quality metal that they would dull quickly, even in cutting soft pine.[46]

Bloomfield told Dearborn that he would move two twelve-pounders from Burlington to Plattsburgh and praised the efforts of Lieutenant Smith of the navy, supporting the acquisition and arming of more vessels: "I hope however, that the spirited young men may receive an accession of gun boats—so as to bear down all attempts of the Enemy to obtain the command of Lake Champlain." His statement is surprising in light of subsequent dealings with the navy.[47]

Here, in early October, was Bloomfield, an army general directing naval activities, ordering the reassignment of naval crews and armament on the same day that Lieutenant Thomas Macdonough, under orders from the secretary of the navy, left Portland for Lake Champlain. Even as he took these naval measures, Bloomfield knew that as winter approached, lake activity would be minimal. He continued to meddle in naval activity even after Macdonough arrived later in the month. He ordered fifty Vermont militiamen to be assigned as crew onboard the sloop *President*, "to do duty whilst Lake Champlain shall be navigable," and instructed navy Lieutenant Smith to position the gunboat *Growler* off Cumberland Head to intercept smugglers.[48]

Eleazer Williams was meeting directly with Dearborn in Albany and always seeking to further the good treatment of his people. Through his negotiations, gunpowder, already in short supply, was now being given to the Indians.[49] Fearing that the British had undermined American efforts to win over the tribe at St. Regis, Dearborn ordered that St. Regis be attacked, a task that would be completed by the end of the month. Williams sought to ensure that those members of the tribe who were sympathetic to the American cause would be spared in such an attack; he ordered his "rangers" to report on the activities of the British, in measure aiding in that effort. He subsequently entered the capture of the first British flag in his journal.[50]

While the 2,400 "undisciplined" regular infantrymen remained at Plattsburgh, Bloomfield assigned border maintenance tasks to the 2,500 militiamen of Vermont and 700 militiamen from New York in orders directing, "The officers & men now on the lines & who shall be ordered to the lines—are to prevent any intercourse with the inhabitants of Canada—or other persons coming from Canada—or attempting to go into Canada—without, or with goods—wares—merchandise, of corn, grain, cattle, Hogs, Beef, Pork, forage, or other articles—of any kind whatsoever."[51]

Macdonough arrived at Whitehall on October 13 and immediately began building what would be his lake fleet: two sloops and several aging and mostly unserviceable gunboats. He wrote to Secretary Hamilton of his desire to rig and move the vessels before the coming ice made it impossible to move north—a formidable task without enough labor. The men who were to be reassigned to his command had not arrived, and as he told Secretary Hamilton, "No seaman are to be procured here." There were difficulties getting craftsmen with the proper skills necessary for the ships' work, and materials were in short supply. Before the end of the month, however, Macdonough would succeed in rigging and outfitting the two sloops with seven guns each—six six-pounders and an eighteen on each—and two gunboats with a twelve-pounder each. The *President*, the most formidable warship on the lake, was, Dearborn insisted, under the control of the army, the idea and practice of which Macdonough could not appreciate. By letter, he explained to Hamilton, "I am strangely deprived of more than half the force in having this vessel in the hands of those, that know not, what to do with her." The regretful unwillingness of the army command to release the other vessels to navy control was not resolved until after Macdonough forwarded his orders from Hamilton to Dearborn.[52]

Bloomfield was concerned about mounting desertions; those who were caught were shot. The situation was growing to be a proverbial "double-edged sword"—i.e., how to attract new recruits if the soldiers you have are running away? The local Plattsburgh paper[53] ran the following recruitment offer:

To men of patriotism and valor.

THE 6th REG. U. S. INFANTRY.

WANTED, a few stout, able bodied young men, from the age of 18 to 33 years, and at least 5 feet 6 inches high, to compleat the said regiment, now stationed at Plattsburgh.

A few of the above description, who wish to acquire HONOR and GLORY in the CAUSE OF THEIR COUNTRY, will receive a LIBERAL BOUNTY by making immediate application to

JOHN J. PLUME,
Lt. & Qt. Mast. 6th Reg. In.

October 1, 1812.

An American infantry recruiting ad in the *Plattsburgh Republican*.

An American bateau. *Author's sketch.*

The buildup of resources at Plattsburgh continued as Bloomfield passed news of British troop strength and movement to Dearborn. Dearborn was contemplating an invasion of Canada. Bloomfield appealed to Governor Galusha of Vermont to fill the militia quota and seek additional volunteers. An additional five hundred of the Vermont militiamen were ordered from Burlington to position themselves in Chazy, and the Sixteenth and Twenty-fifth regiments were dispatched to Plattsburgh by batteaux.[54]

Shortly after the beginning of November, Bloomfield issued, by secret orders, the plans to invade Canada. Champlain was to be the assembly point for the massing army: "The US Troops & all the Vermont Militia will be at Champlain on Sunday the 17th & on the 18th Enter Canada." All tents and baggage were to be left at Champlain and Chazy. With six days of rations, the troops were to proceed north with only "what they carry on their backs." Eleazer Williams related Bloomfield's orders that boats be repaired and wagons readied for the campaign. Troops from St. Regis were recalled to Champlain but were ordered to depart "unencumbered with any baggage."[55]

Dearborn arrived in the middle of November to take command. Williams speaks of attending a "council of war" on November 20 and the probability of success in light of the feelings of border Canadians, forced into service, who were unwilling to join the conflict. Yet he was disturbed by the uncertainty of the American plans.[56] The beginnings of a poorly planned November fiasco had been set in motion.

With the arrival of the artillery, the American forces moved north. Some of the militia would not move across the border. The force moved slowly and saw very few British. Without tents, they slept on the ground, unsheltered, in the cold, damp and snow. Dr. Beaumont described the condition as "destitute of covering save a Blanket or two…lying upon the cold, wet ground, with only a fire before their tents, for two, three or four weeks." A company under the command of Colonel Zebulon Pike did attack the British guard force at LaColle, only to be fired upon by another American company. Everest relates the result: "Two dead, thirteen wounded, and five missing, most of the casualties resulting from their own fire." The American forces, cold, wet, short on rations and other supplies, returned to Champlain and went on to Plattsburgh.[57]

The *Plattsburgh Republican* published the following account on December 4, 1812:

> *The army which lately marched to the north, returned to this place on Mon the 23rd November and have gone into winter quarters. The 9th, 11th, 21st and 25th regiments have gone to Burlington, the 6th, 15th, and 46th remain and are building huts for the winter, the light artillery and dragoons have returned to Albany.*

By December 8, the American Northern Army was preparing to quarter for the colder months, and the New York and Vermont militias were returning to their homes. Before leaving to winter in Vermont, Eleazer Williams spoke with General Mooers about the use of the Indian Rangers through the winter, and arrangements were made to issue provisions to the "Squads of Indians" at French Mills. Thomas Macdonough detoured to Middletown to marry, returning with his new wife, Lucy, for a Burlington, Vermont winter. Dr. Beaumont remarked that the men were still "in tents with small fires in front"; he was administering treatments for "Dysentery, Pleurisy and Peripneumony." Winter conditions and arrangements for the navy's fleet were communicated to Secretary Hamilton.[58]

"Winter quarters" for the two thousand or so troops left at Plattsburgh did not mean solid, comfortable housing. As there were no huts built, they slept on the ground in tents. They set about building several hundred log shelters in the beginning of December, a month described by Dr. Mann as "severely cold."

Pike's Cantonment. *Author's sketch.*

Everest describes the unpleasant conditions of the time in the language of Dr. William Beaumont: "The very woods ring with coughing and groaning." Beaumont relates the death rate of the Eleventh Regiment: "Behold the gasping, gasping Mortals, how they die! Twenty-six in the course of two weeks out of four hundred."

According to Dr. Mann, nearly one-third of the troops suffered from measles, and over the winter, some two hundred would die in the cantonment at Plattsburgh. On the hillside by the Saranac River, two to five men were said to be dying each day from complications due to dysentery and pneumonia.[59]

Thus, the close of the year 1812 saw a "Valley Forge" situation in Plattsburgh. The Revolutionary War experience of Washington's troops could be viewed as a parallel—but less severe. The southern Pennsylvania winter of 1777–78 was described as "moderate."[60]

3
Forces Build (1813)

Early January was snowy and cold, as described by Eleazer Williams. The forces of Plattsburgh under Zebulon Pike were just finishing their huts after sleeping in tents from snowy mid-December. Survival was foremost. Williams left Plattsburgh in a sleigh for St. Regis, stopping at Roberts's Inn in Chateaugay. He met with his rangers and sent word to Plattsburgh of enemy movements at St. Johns, Chamblee and Cornwall and a major buildup at Kingston. An attack at Sackets Harbor was forming.

While at Roberts's Inn, a traveler from the lines to the north spoke of reinforcements arriving at Isle aux Noix and an Indian party at LaColle. Williams made arrangements for continued support of the Indians at St. Regis, who had expressed the desire to remain neutral. He also heard of British orders for his arrest. An ailing Williams returned to Plattsburgh on January 6.[1]

At Plattsburgh, Williams met with General Mooers and was treated by military doctors. Williams's was not the only illness. The sad state of Pike's troops was the subject of Williams's journal entry for January 10:

> *It is to be regretted that the northern army is in a sick condition—ten or twelve men are daily buried. Dysentery and diarrhea are the principal diseases, which are often combined with typhus fever. Colonel Pike, who commands this post, is doing all in his power to assuage the sufferings of his troops, by making the medical department do its duty—the noted Dr. Mann being at its head.*[2]

Across the lake in Vermont, Thomas Macdonough was making plans to fit his fleet to meet the improvements the British had made to their vessels over the winter. He wrote to the newly appointed navy secretary, Jones, of the British plan for lake superiority in the coming season and of his desire to better the U.S. fleet to meet the threat. He requested more able-bodied seamen and carpenters and twelve additional cannons for his ships. In a separate letter to Mr. Goldsborough of the Naval Office, he addressed problems with purchasing supplies and provisions, telling Goldsborough that his men, "a sailing master, purser, five midshipmen & twenty two men…are in this ice country almost destitute of clothing."[3]

Williams's rangers reported to him in early February that the British were concentrating troops at Kingston, across from Sackets Harbor. Very little local army activity took place that month, with the exception of Major Forsythe's successful surprise raid on Elizabethtown (across the St. Lawrence from Ogdensburg). In the coming weeks, Williams's rangers would report that additional troops were arriving at Montreal from Quebec. He communicated the information to General Dearborn and alerted the commander at Sackets Harbor.[4]

Acknowledging the threat to Sackets Harbor, Dearborn ordered Zebulon Pike to move westward. Pike ordered snowshoes[5] and requested a report of troops and supplies at Chateaugay and French Mills; he planned to rest his troops at these points on the way. He reported to General Dearborn that he would immediately send four hundred men (with twenty-four rounds of ammunition and fifteen days' rations each) as far as Ogdensburg. These men would bring with them a howitzer and a three-pound cannon on a sleigh. He would send an additional four hundred men and ten pieces of

"Captain of United States Infantry, 1813."
From How Canada Was Held for the Empire.

artillery as soon as 150 sleighs with teams and enough grain to support them could be gathered.[6]

The threat grew more intense as Pike learned that two companies of artillery with eighteen cannons moved from Montreal for the west. British troop strength near Kingston had swelled to over 1,900. Forsythe, having been driven from Ogdensburg by the British on the twenty-first, was ordered to return westward. Forsythe's men successfully attacked Elizabethtown and were on their way to Sackets Harbor before Pike's first troops departed Plattsburgh. Communicating to General Dearborn, Pike informed the general of his contingency plans: if the British forces were indeed in Kingston or to the west of it, his troops would continue their march from Ogdensburg to Sackets Harbor, creating a force approximately equal to the British force there. Once he arrived at Sackets Harbor, if the British had departed for the west, Pike would attack Kingston.[7]

On March 3, after conferring with Eleazer Williams regarding an appropriate route, Pike departed Plattsburgh with one-third of his command in sleighs or wearing snowshoes. On the seventh and eighth, Pike ordered Colonel Pearce and Captain Brooks's artillery at Plattsburgh and Major Whitlock at Champlain to follow. He cautioned the officers of the cold and the danger of troops suffering frostbite (a situation made worse by a general state of intoxication among the troops). He informed Generals Chandler and Dearborn of his orders and requisitioned supplies and ammunition as could be spared from Plattsburgh and Champlain.[8]

From Sackets Harbor, Pike sent word to General Woolsey at Plattsburgh that the British General Prevost had stalled. He complained to Woolsey that among the six thousand regulars, militiamen and volunteers gathered, there was not a single blacksmith. A near state of chaos existed when there was not enough money to pay the militia or the teamsters who had transported troops from Plattsburgh; Pike acted quickly, borrowing the funds from his officers. He requested that Woolsey order the First Brigade of the Northern Army to proceed "without unnecessary delay with arms & accoutrements as soon as possible" and that the general come to Sackets Harbor with the regimental farrier or one that could be found.[9]

In mid-March, as Dearborn departed for Sackets Harbor, Pike reported the continued fortification and troop buildup at Kingston and indications that spring was approaching—i.e., several horses had fallen through the thinning lake ice. He ordered one hundred pairs of pistols, 333 swords, two twelve-pounders and all stores from Plattsburgh. "Every man of the 13th Brigade who are able to move," he ordered, "will all be forwarded on by

Detachments with all possible dispatch." At the time, he had six thousand troops and would call for an additional four thousand. Informing the traveling General Dearborn of his attack plan, Pike proposed a checking action at Brockport and an artillery attack at York; the major force would concentrate on Kingston from two directions. With such a plan, Pike believed he could "cut off the upper province entirely" if accomplished before summer. He foretold the arrival of massive troop reinforcements from Europe, telling the general that there could eventually be twenty thousand men at Montreal.

On April 5, Pike learned of his promotion to brigadier general and replied with his formal acceptance through General John Armstrong. Eleazer Williams's Rangers reported that the British were concerned about an invasion, the result of Pike's growing force and Dearborn's arrival.[10]

Williams reflected on the situation from his government-paid quarters at Charlotte, Vermont:

> *The two great contending parties appear to be, for the present, in a tranquil state; preparing, however, for a severe and blody* [sic] *conflict. O, that God would be pleased to put an end to all wars…I am again called on by the war department to perform certain duties which are delicate and dangerous in the extreme. I have issued my orders to the whole corps of Rangers, to be in readiness to perform the duties assigned to each of them. This is a terrible and efficient corps in the service of the government. No movement is made by the enemy but is known to them. They are constantly, as it were, within the enemy's camp, or on every side of them. This corps was embodied by Col. Isaac Clark, of the 11th Regt., in connection with the secretary of war. As to my position with them, my order is final. No appeal can be made from it. They are constantly exposed to martial law and to death. Their courage, bravery, and fidelity save them, the war department often applauds their daring conduct, and rewards their services with high wages. They are faithful to the government. My orders they are always ready to obey, at which I have often been surprised. When I am absent from the department, Major-Gen. Mooers takes my place. He was an officer during the Revolution, under his uncle, Col. Hazen.[11]*

In the middle of April, Williams was summoned to Albany for several meetings with Governor Tompkins. After reporting on recent enemy movements, Williams was asked to comment on a secret communication received from the War Department. His journal reflects Tompkins's satisfaction for the efforts of the rangers and notes "the quarter-master-general has once more replenished the secret service money." Williams returned to Vermont, moving on to Middleburg, where a paymaster joined his company; the Indians were being regularly paid and reimbursed for expenses.[12]

On May 1, Thomas Macdonough reported to Secretary Jones of his arrival at Plattsburgh and the fleet under his command: *President, Growler, Eagle* and two gunboats. By the sixth, the alterations that were necessary to ready the vessels for service were completed, and carronades were being mounted. Macdonough lacked a purser and a surgeon's mate, but he was confident that his fleet was now superior to that which the British would put on the lake for the season. Macdonough was eager to proceed north to the lines.[13]

On May 15, a somber Eleazer Williams wrote in his journal of receiving news of the death of Zebulon Pike during the successful attack on Toronto: "I lament the loss of the amiable and brave Col. Pike." He reflected also on the fate of his rangers if they should be caught—and the fate of any spy of the British who might be caught also. They would, he wrote, "suffer death in accordance with martial-law." Four days later, Williams met with Macdonough and the other officers at Plattsburgh in a council of war. The campaigns of 1813 were gaining momentum. In the next several days, Williams's rangers would report British troop movements toward Kingston: Oswego and Sackets Harbor were the perceived targets.

In Plattsburgh, veterans of the Revolution were forming their company of exempts in anticipation of a future defense. The rangers subsequently informed Williams (on the twenty-ninth) that Sackets Harbor had indeed been attacked, unsuccessfully, but with significant loss to the American forces. Perhaps, as Williams reflected, the information provided by his rangers had been instrumental in an early alert of forces at Sackets Harbor and their ability to repel the attacking British.[14]

The end of May and the beginning of June proved frustrating for Macdonough. One of his gunboats overturned in heavy winds, entering Plattsburgh Bay, the entire crew thrown into the icy spring waters of Lake Champlain. Several days later, the sloops *Growler* and *Eagle*, under the command of Lieutenant Sidney Smith, proceeded north to chase British gunboats near Isle aux Noix.

Eleazer Williams took notice of "heavy cannonading to the north at about 10 o'clock" on the morning of June 3. Smith had, unfortunately, and against the advice of his pilot, permitted his gunboats to be caught in a narrow channel by currents and the early June winds. Under fire by the British, with both vessels bottomed in shallow waters, Smith and his crews were captured, with one death and nineteen injured. The British would refit the vessels with eleven guns, including long, pivot-mounted eighteen-pounders forward. The captured vessels' names were changed to *Shannon* and *Broke*.

Macdonough immediately reported the loss to Secretary Jones and requested that he be able to purchase two replacement sloops to remain effective in countering the British fleet. The new vessels would need cannons to outfit them; none was available locally. Macdonough asked Jones for twenty eighteen-pounder carronades and one thousand grapeshot cylinders. Being suddenly short of crew, Macdonough requested "three experienced Lieutenants, six midshipmen, three gunners, thirty seamen and twenty ordinary seamen."[15]

On June 11, revenue agent Peter Sailly wrote to the quartermaster general that a small British force, under a flag of truce, had reached Cumberland Head by water before being noticed. The British now knew that there was no defense in place. Most of the army was deployed west; a smaller force remained at Burlington, and Macdonough had taken his naval fleet to Burlington. Sailly wrote:

> *Thus Plattsburgh, its arsenal, its unarmed block house, its public stores are all at the mercy of the enemy. It is hardly worth the while to mention its inhabitants. It would seem that since the departure of the troops for Sacket's* [sic] *Harbor, they have not been thought worthy of protection…Many of the inhabitants of this village have packed up their effects and keep horses ready to depart on the first sight of an enemy.*[16]

Sailly's communication and alarm at the conditions went unanswered.

The remainder of the month of June and the entire month of July were building months for the American army and navy. While Plattsburgh was largely unprotected, Burlington's military presence grew to some four thousand. July also saw the coming of a new Northern Army commander, General Wade Hampton, a man who would quickly become almost universally disliked. The short-tempered, sixty-something general came to the Champlain Valley from previous assignments at Norfolk and New Orleans. Eleazer Williams immediately noted strange behaviors upon meeting Hampton and termed him "an enemy to his species."

By the middle of July, Williams's rangers detected preparations at St. Johns and Isle aux Noix, which Williams believed to indicate that some British action was imminent. Knowing that Plattsburgh was virtually unprotected, and after corroborating the reports of his rangers, Williams interpreted and reported the indications evidenced north of the lines as an impending attack. Having anticipated the next British movements, he met with Hampton on the thirtieth. Hampton, planning an invasion of Canada, paid no heed to Williams's warning. Tenuous relations would persist until Hampton's unceremonious and hasty withdrawal from Plattsburgh in the coming fall.[17]

At Burlington with his fleet, Macdonough purchased another sloop and spent the month outfitting it to be ready by the end of July. Short of personnel and disappointed by the navy's personnel movements, he manned two gunboats with army troops. While the sloop itself was completed within his expected schedule, he was frustrated by the lack of requested guns. There was a bright spot in the month for Macdonough, however: he was named master commandant.[18]

With Macdonough's fleet in a state of repair at Burlington and the preoccupied Hampton planning to move on Canada, the British colonel John Murray saw an opportunity and moved a force south on the lake. With the two captured and refitted sloops, gunboats and scores of bateaux under the command of Captain Pring, the British flotilla passed Champlain on the thirtieth and headed for Plattsburgh.

Eleazer Williams, on his way to Plattsburgh, was met at Grand Isle with news of the impending British raid. He returned immediately to Charlotte; his fears had been realized. With the crack of a cannon early in the morning on the thirty-first, the British force of about eight hundred under the command of Colonel Murray landed at Plattsburgh. It was met by the small force of remaining regulars, local militia and veteran exempts. The Americans quickly dispersed in the face of the larger force and the promise that only public government property would be disturbed or destroyed. Murray ordered that the arsenal and the commissary store be emptied of any useful supplies and had the store and other public buildings set on fire or torn down. The task accomplished, Murray moved west to burn the hutted encampment area where Pike had wintered his troops into the previous spring:—"recently erected and capable of accommodating from four to five thousand men." The deliberate movements of the British within the village that day were said to be the result of a local collaborator's map indicating specific targets of military significance. According to the reminiscence of James Bailey, the map was discovered quite by accident as it fell from Murray's hat.

Mr. Gilliland, the military storekeeper, retrieved the map without notice by the British. A local, Mr. Ackley, "was subsequently arrested and sent to

Albany for trial." With no witnesses appearing, the trial did not proceed, and Ackley is said to have quietly moved his family to Quebec. Peter Sailly wrote to the secretary of the treasury of the government damage estimate at Plattsburgh ($30,000). The damage was suffered without a shot having been fired, while just twenty miles away, four thousand U.S. troops under the command of General Hampton sat at Burlington. Hampton, warned well in advance of the probability of an attack on Plattsburgh, ignored requests for assistance. Eleazer Williams would later report to the secretary of war and Governor Tompkins of the Plattsburgh fiasco and Hampton's disregard of the situation (after having been informed of the conditions). Williams's journal speaks of his "fears in regard to General Hampton."[19]

By ten o'clock in the morning, Murray's troops had sacked and burned Plattsburgh. Contrary to the promises made just hours earlier, some local citizens saw their personal property stolen, damaged, or destroyed. Henry DeLord's house was occupied by British officers and the carpet ruined. (Almost a year later, amid an impending American invasion of Canada, an apologetic Major Ritter of the British Sixth Light Infantry, in an act of gentlemanly civility, forwarded a bale of carpeting to DeLord with his apologies.)

With the mission completed, Murray dispatched the bulk of the forces to return north. They did so, but not without leaving a trail of pillage and destruction at the northern end of Cumberland Head, Point Au Roche, Chazy and Swanton in Vermont. Murray ordered the sloops and a gunboat toward Burlington.

Pring entered Burlington Harbor and began to fire on the merchant vessels and the shore battery. Macdonough, in relating the incident to Secretary Jones, told of the British capturing two vessels, burning one and leaving only after meeting with fire from his anchored vessels and the heavy pieces on the hilltop battery.

Macdonough again requested additional officers and sailors to meet the growing naval threat. He gave as evidence his inability to meet the British flotilla due to lack of personnel. Pring returned to the northern lines unmolested.[20]

On August 6, a young soldier by the name of James Daugherty became the first person to be executed in the county of Clinton. He had been tried earlier in the year for the death of Ethan Bradley, a boy from the Salmon River settlement who had been delivering hay to the winter cantonment area.[21]

The second week of August arrived with Eleazer Williams being "politely requested to pay no regard to General Hampton's rough language."[22] We can assume that with the War Department's focus on invading Canada, Hampton couldn't be immediately replaced. Williams apparently agreed to help where he could. Hampton's distaste for Williams and the use of Indians in the coming campaign was evident in his August 19 communication with General Mooers. He questioned Dearborn's instructions on the use of the Indians, instead requesting that Mooers have them stand ready for duty at the beginning of September, but under strict control, for use "by way of trial." Hampton thought it proper that Indians be used to set fire to the abatis-ridden northern frontier as soon as the weather dried and there were strong south winds. Williams continued to forward information to Hampton and impressed upon General Mooers the loyalty of the native chiefs. Hampton repeated his objections to Mooers on August 29:

> *Of the Indian affairs I know nothing & I am resolved not to know; nor will I have anything to do with them…If they are good for any thing, they shall be paid the wages of the United States troops, but they must clothe themselves. If they are good for nothing they can be discharged.*

On September 5, Mooers, for Eleazer Williams's part as the Indian agent and in accordance with the instructions from General Dearborn, paid the man's yearly salary of $591.40 and $100.00 in expenses for his 755 miles of travels between Greenbush, St. Regis and Plattsburgh. Contrary to Hampton's desire—and, it can be assumed, at the direction of Governor Tompkins—Mooers continued to pay for Indian clothing. On that day, Mooers paid an additional $477.73 for Williams's clothing, provisions, supplies, Indian services and interpretation.[23]

In early September, with Macdonough's fleet ready, Hampton felt confident to move. On the sixth, Williams was asked by Hampton to "reconnoitre the position at La Cole river, and examine the possibility of his penetrating, with the army, from Chautegay Four Corners into Canada." Williams's journal entry of that day notes Governor Tompkins's lack of confidence in Hampton. On the eighth, Macdonough arrived at Plattsburgh from Burlington and proceeded north without incident.

Hampton met with Mooers and Williams and reported to Secretary of War Armstrong that he would soon be ready; General Izard arrived at Plattsburgh on the sixteenth. The movement of American troops toward the border to the west was about to begin.[24]

For the remainder of the month of September, Hampton sat waiting for provisions and supplies to arrive and for the completion of a roadway over which to transport his forces. On October 4, he reported to Armstrong that he had eight six-pounders, one twelve-pounder and one howitzer at the ready and that the roadway was complete. He still waited for bread, flour, salted provisions, musket cartridges and cannon powder sufficient for a sixty-day excursion. Even though he was not ready to move, he called for militia and volunteer participation in a "petty war, or invasion of the lines, at or near Lake Champlain."[25]

Hampton moved in early October toward Chateaugay, and Prevost moved a sizeable force south from Kingston. The British to the north of Plattsburgh, for their part, answered Hampton's movements by sailing to Champlain along the shoreline, confiscating every vessel they found and orchestrating several raids into Champlain. They were said to have completed two new row galleys carrying twenty-four-pounders; in Plattsburgh, two American row galleys were in construction.

On the ninth, Hampton and Williams, in a contentious meeting, discussed Williams's being requested to assist General Wilkinson outside Ogdensburg. After first objecting to the movement, Hampton grudgingly agreed. Hampton told Williams of his plans for attack; Williams suggested that, because of enemy movements and the strength of forces, he might be successful in an attack by way of LaColle and L'Acadia. The idea was rejected. In the latter part of the month, Hampton began to move his troops north. They were met with significant resistance, causing him to recall the force. At a council of war with Hampton and his officers, Williams again presented information regarding troop movement and strength to the north.

"There was great discord in their views with regard to their military operations," Williams wrote in his journal. Trouble was brewing in the Hampton ranks and among Wilkinson's American force to the west.

On the eleventh, at Crysler's Farm, Wilkinson's forces were soundly defeated, and Hampton's troops returned to Plattsburgh. The following was within the text of a general order issued from British headquarters at LaChine on November 13:

James Wilkinson. *From the* Pictorial Field Book of the War of 1812.

The Governor in Chief and Commander of the Forces has the satisfaction to announce to the troops, that the corps of observation with the division of Gun-boats, which he had ordered from Kingston to follow the movement of the enemy's army under Maj. Gen Wilkinson, and to be placed under the command of Lieut. Col. Morrison, of the 89ᵗʰ regiment, has completely defeated a large division of the American army, consisting of cavalry, riflemen and infantry, exceeding Four Thousand men, which attacked it on the 11 inst. Near Crysler's about 20 miles above Cornwall, taking from the enemy 1 field piece, six pounder, and 400 prisoners. [26]

For the remainder of November, Williams reported on the favorable conditions, still existing, for an invasion to the north from Plattsburgh. He felt that the Canadian sentiment was such that the local militia would be reluctant to engage the American forces (the Canadians were said to have been forced into service). The event never happened, and Williams left on November 29 to winter in Charlotte. Williams wrote in his journal with a sense of relief, "The enemy is rejoicing to see that our armies are going into winter quarters. Peace be with him."[27]

On December 2, as a cold northern winter began to set in, Williams learned that orders had been issued in the last days of November that called for the arrest of General Hampton. Hampton evaded the action through the advance word of friends; he resigned. With Governor Tompkins keeping alive the hope of a winter attack on Canada at Prescott or Montreal, Williams traveled often to Albany through the month, passing information to the governor of the movements of the British and conditions north of the border.[28]

Perhaps at the urging of Peter Sailly, Macdonough received orders from Secretary Jones to prepare to build fifteen additional gunboats. Sailly's communication with Jones stressed the need for vessels with shallow draft, "sufficiently flat at bottom," which could more easily navigate the lake and the connecting rivers. Jones directed that Macdonough plan for vessels "75 feet long and 15 wide, to carry a long 24 and a 42 pound carronade, row 40 oars, and drawing but 22 inches of water, with all on board." Whether Sailly's prompting influenced Jones's action, Jones had seen to it that additional supplies and ordnance be placed at Albany for Macdonough to draw on before the winter's ice formed.[29]

The year's end brought a peaceful, if not cold, completion to local involvement in the 1813 campaigns. Captain Ezra Turner cautioned the local militia "to pay due attention to their arms and ammunition, that they may be found fit for service at a moment's warning for any emergency; for we know not at what hour the thief may come."[30]

4

Anticipation and Alarm
(January to June 1814)

As nervous New York militia members received their pay throughout the month of January, they spoke of local community concerns for certain actions taken within Canada just north of Plattsburgh; they sensed an impending attack. Imploring General Wilkinson, the *Plattsburgh Republican* offered the observation:

> *For a short time past, the enemy have strictly and rightly prohibited all intercourse with the interior of their country, and have entirely prevented from passing, smugglers, and other persons who have heretofore been permitted to pass and repass, without interruption.*

Williams's rangers did point to some activity in the area of Isle aux Noix but did not report with alarm. He noted that "troops here are at their ease. They have now good quarters." Regardless, there was a bumbling "secret expedition" from Plattsburgh that resulted in the death of a soldier by a surprised American picket guard stationed near the border.[1]

Wilkinson did order a company of dragoons (cavalry) from Burlington and a detachment of infantry from Chateaugay to Plattsburgh. He followed shortly with additional troops after ordering that the provisions and supplies from French Mills be forwarded to Plattsburgh. Eleazer Williams received instructions from the Department of War that he was to proceed to French Mills; he watched as the winter campaign "ended without accomplishing the object."[2]

There were brief border skirmishes north of Plattsburgh through the month, but no mass movement of troops materialized. Nevertheless,

Wilkinson requested that Williams's rangers reconnoiter the situation at Isle aux Noix and at LaColle.[3]

Perhaps the most interesting events of January were the court-martial sentences carried out at Plattsburgh. For cowardice, abandonment of his post and unofficer-like conduct, a Lieutenant Gates was suspended from command for three months and confined to the post. A Lieutenant Barret was tried for cowardice, unofficer-like and ungentleman-like conduct and desertion; he was cashiered, with his sword broken over his head.[4]

February began with a significant buildup of American troops at French Mills. Additional provisions were ordered with the condition: "The Contractor will send Forward ten days flour to Chataguay as soon as possible; and with respect to the deposit of provisions at Malone will accelerate its transport to the point of destination." Wilkinson left for French Mills with the Twenty-ninth Regiment but would return shortly. According to Benjamin Mooers, Wilkinson had taken comfortable quarters with the DeLord family (he did return on the sixteenth). At French Mills, a sense of alarm was building; the American forces were placed in a state of alert and were being spread across the North Country on foot and in sleigh. Two regiments, a detachment of the Fifth Rifle Corps, a battalion of the Fifth Artillery and a company of the Second Artillery were ordered to Sackets Harbor. The movement orders

Alexander Macomb. *From the* Pictorial Field Book of the War of 1812.

contained instructions that they were not to depart without any man "whose life will not be immediately endangered by the Journey." Major Forsythe's corps was to "guard the pass on the Salmon River." Colonel Alexander Macomb, soon General Macomb, was to march a company to reinforce Plattsburgh (Wilkinson had just left with a regiment). The company of the Second Artillery at Plattsburgh was to march for Sackets Harbor. Eleazer Williams, apparently not having been informed by Wilkinson, witnessed the flurry of force movements and believed that an invasion of Canada was near.[5]

Plattsburgh would soon see a battalion of light artillery and a detachment of riflemen arrive from French Mills. Amidst the confusing transfers of units, the local paper reported, "immense quantities of Military Stores, &c. have arrived at this place, from French Mills. It is understood that several regiments have marched for Sacket's Harbor, and that the main body of the army will be located at this place, after the public property shall have been removed from French Mills."

After a number of vessels and their supplies were transferred to Plattsburgh, the barracks and the remaining boats at French Mills were destroyed. A council of war was held in Plattsburgh to discuss invasion plans—LaColle Mill would be the first attack. Macomb, with the Sixth and Fifteenth Regiments and the sick, was ordered to Burlington.[6]

On the evening of February 19, as the British ventured across the St. Lawrence to the abandoned French Mills, the officers at Plattsburgh were entertained at a ball at Israel Green's Hotel. The gaiety was short lived as news reached Plattsburgh of the British entering Chateaugay with eight pieces of artillery. It was presumed that the British were following the American movements; Wilkinson departed to meet them. General Macomb was ordered to return to Plattsburgh. Eleazer Williams's rangers delivered information concerning the status of the forces at St. Johns, Chamblee, La Prairie and Montreal.[7]

At the end of the month, Thomas Macdonough received word from Secretary Jones that a contract had been entered into with Noah Brown of New York City to "launch a ship of 24 guns on Lake Champlain, in 60 days, and presuming that the alleged fact of the enemy having a ship of that class in great forwardness." Macdonough was told to proceed immediately with the purchase of the 120-foot vessel under construction as a steamboat at Vergennes.[8]

March started with an enforcement of trade restrictions across the borders of upper New York and Vermont. The Plattsburgh paper trumpeted, "Smugglers look out, as you will soon see the fur fly." The British responded by reinforcing St. Johns and Isle aux Noix. The American forces made final preparations and received from Eleazer Williams updated information regarding the state of the area near LaColle Mill. Williams urged an immediate move against the stone mill before the ice went out.

The mill was built on an island; without the ice, attack routes would be frustrated. He advised that the building of redoubts in frozen ground was futile if General Wilkinson contemplated a siege and that ordnance had to be sufficient to batter the walls of the mill—e.g., eighteen-pounders. The general took little of Williams's suggestions, and an order was given to march north on the seventh. Williams informed the War Department of his advice to the general.[9]

Macdonough proceeded as directed and notified Secretary Jones of Brown's progress. With news of the British building galleys, Macdonough began the process of building his own vessels. He reported that the steamboat would be "purchased, finished and fitted."[10]

Much happened during the third week of March. Major Forsythe moved across the border unopposed and into the area near Isle aux Noix, all surgeons and surgeons' mates were ordered into service, and rifle companies and cavalry were ordered near the border. General Mooers took time to purchase a property in the Village of Plattsburgh at what is now the corner of Bridge and Pike Streets.[11]

On March 26, the day on which British sergeant William Baker of the 103rd Regiment of Infantry was executed as a spy in Plattsburgh, the local paper also held news of a major naval buildup near Sackets Harbor: "We shall look to lake Ontario in a few short weeks with much anxiety, as presenting the most interesting scene that this war has yet produced." The 4,000-man American force was poised at Champlain in preparation for moving on LaColle Mill; the British were advancing 2,500 men from St. Johns and Isle aux Noix. Just four days later, the order to enter Canada was made. The American troops were to have five days' rations and sixty rounds; any man who would not go forward on command was to be shot.[12]

Wilkinson's American force led by Forsythe's rifle company, the Thirtieth and Thirty-first Regiments and part of the Eleventh did march north on the morning of March 30. They were slowed by tree-obstructed, snow-covered roadways. General Macomb, with infantry and other reserves, followed. Wilkinson occupied the woods near the mill and set a battery of three twelve-pounders to fire on it. Shortly after, British reinforcements arrived.

The Thirteenth Regiment from St. Johns, a company of grenadiers (troops armed with grenades), and a company of voltiguers attempted to silence

Wilkinson's guns; they failed but inflicted serious casualties on the American force. The ice had begun to clear, and Captain Pring moved his vessel and gunboats into the mouth of the LaColle River, firing on the American forces and landing supplies for the mill. Wilkinson had waited too long before attacking and had disregarded Eleazer Williams's advice about the size of the artillery necessary for a siege. The British anticipated the American move and were successful in reinforcing the mill. Wilkinson's cannons had little effect on the mill walls. The event ended in defeat for the Americans: 104 killed and wounded; the British lost 56. Wilkinson withdrew his force toward Champlain, the focus changing from invasion to protection—of Plattsburgh. In a defensive mode now, Wilkinson sent Macomb to Burlington as protection for the major stores amassed there. Eleazer Williams recorded the news of Wilkinson's defeat in his journal, reflecting on the two embarrassing campaigns that Wilkinson had orchestrated "without a military eye and due preparation."[13]

With the northern end of the lake free of ice, the British began to move south. A report of several vessels anchored at Rouses Point and a large number of bateaux gathered at St. Johns caused Macdonough, powerless to effect any naval defense, to write to Peter Sailly on April 6 from Vergennes, Vermont. The village of Plattsburgh was in danger if the British seized and sunk vessels in the mouth of the Saranac. Such a barricade would effectively close off access to the village. Macdonough suggested the placement of a battery at the mouth of the river. Five batteries were subsequently built on the order of General Macomb who called for furnaces to be constructed for use in heating shot. Huts were being built on the southern side of the Saranac River, and formal camp rules were directed—e.g., provisioners' shipments would be searched, no unauthorized personnel would be permitted to enter, soldiers were to see to it that they relieved themselves at the assigned vaults (latrines) and, besides normal rations, no liquor was permitted within the encampment.[14]

Wilkinson set a picket guard and dragoons on the northern end of Cumberland Head to view the lake. Macomb ordered that the picket be furnished with rockets to be fired immediately upon the sighting of an enemy vessel; the dragoons were to ride immediately to headquarters with details of the sighting. On April 10, Wilkinson banned gambling and the use of cards and dice, insisting that the troops' leisure time be concentrated on military discipline, instruction and readiness. We can only assume that the order was obeyed grudgingly and that word of these latest edicts reached the War Department rather hastily. Eleazer Williams received word that Wilkinson would soon be replaced by General Izard. An order was given by the secretary of war that Wilkinson be arrested and brought before a court of inquiry; command would be given to General Macomb in the meantime.[15]

Macdonough's ship, *Saratoga*, was launched on the eleventh, built in forty days. Its keel was said to be 130 feet with a beam of 37 feet, displacing over 250 tons and to mount six long twenty-four-, eight forty-two- and fourteen thirty-two-pound carronades. Though afloat, the ship could not be rigged or fitted because the equipment requisitioned from Troy had not arrived, the delay caused by still-impassable roads. Macdonough again wrote to Secretary Jones of his need for manpower. Ironically, the Quebec papers of the day note that British sailors were not arriving in sufficient numbers.[16]

Across the Atlantic, Bonaparte was defeated, and Britain began the withdrawal of its troops from Spain. The situation in Canada, heretofore only a distraction, would now become a priority. The Falmouth paper in England reported on April 19 that part of Lord Wellington's army was "already under orders for America."[17]

Tensions increased throughout the month. Major Forsythe (soon, Lieutenant Colonel Forsythe) and his rifle company were ordered from Chazy into barracks erected at the Dead Creek, just north of the village between it and Cumberland Head. The artillery was authorized to conduct target-practice exercises, and each man's musket, ammunition and supplies were ordered to be inspected and placed in proper order for turn out "upon the least alarm." In the face of coming conflict, desertions increased, and military justice was swift. Three soldiers—Charles Stewart, John Sennet and Joseph Curtis—were tried by court-martial and sentenced to death (they were executed at Plattsburgh on May 9).[18]

On the twenty-third, as Wilkinson left the North Country and Eleazer Williams headed for the northern lines to follow enemy movements, Macomb assumed command. The London papers were reporting the movement of ten thousand of Wellington's army to America. Macomb recalled the Fourth and Tenth Regiments from Burlington with orders that all soldiers whose health would not be endangered by the movement be removed to Plattsburgh and that all public boats (bateaux) stored for the previous winter be collected.[19]

At the end of the month, Macdonough reported to Jones the *Saratoga*'s progress: rigged, sails ready to be bent, quarters ready, carriages completed and awaiting gun. The new row galleys were in a similar state. The steamboat, he told Jones, could not "pass through the lake without something happening to her"; replacement parts were not available locally. He told Jones that the British efforts were comparable but that he would attempt to beat them to the lake. Jones did not doubt that Macdonough would command the lake and conveyed that thought to Madison.[20]

In London during the first week of May, the papers were abuzz with assumptions, assumptions that would prove to be without merit. The *Courier* published the following:

> *A very general expectation appears to be entertained, that the Americans, when appraised of the recent changes in Europe, will cashier Mr. Madison...the Americans may follow the example of France...& return to the protection of the former sovereign.*

Likewise, the following appeared in *Corbett's Register*:

> *As to the state of opinions in America, it appears, that, having heard of the low state of Napoleon's affairs, the people there were counting with confidence, on an immediate peace. They had not then heard of the actual dethronement of Napoleon, and of the consequent language of our public prints accompanied with statements of troops immediately to be sent off to America. What effect these will produce in the minds of the people and of the government there, I know not; but, so slowly do they generally move, it is not probable, that the troops will meet with any like an army to oppose them. The Americans have no experienced officers. They have no discipline. They will, too, I dare say, think, that because they beat England in the last war, they can do it again...They will, if our troops really should land in their country, have to contend with those who have defeated French armies, with skill of all sorts; experience in the men as well as the officers; with courage, discipline, and the habit of victory. All these will require something more than the Americans have yet thought of.*[21]

Upon taking command of the regiments at Plattsburgh in the first week of May, General Izard ordered that the men "wear their clothes and accoutrements night and day" from May 11, this being ordered to speed their assembly in case of attack. Musicians were ordered to practice seven hours a day in preparation for the coming engagements. On the thirteenth, Eleazer Williams had his first meeting with General Izard. On the following day, Izard declared that all officers were to have a copy of Von Steuben's blue book, the principles of which were to be followed regarding the "police and duties in the camp" and for parade. On the same day, an exchange of prisoners was effected that yielded the return of 250 privates and the following 10 officers:

Captain Gustavus Loomis, First Artillery
Lieutenants James Stewart, John S. Williamson, H. Fredericks, Littelton Johnson and Adam Peck
Sailing Masters James Loomis and James Trant
Mate Samuel Osgood
Midshipman W.N. Monteath.[22]

Pring moved up the lake with a brig, three sloops, thirteen galleys and a detachment of marines (on the way, taking every vessel found on the shoreline). Passing Plattsburgh, he headed for the Vermont shoreline, stopping at Providence Island off the southwest end of the mid-lake Hero Island. The Americans assumed that Pring, being first on the lake, would head for Vergennes to blockade Otter Creek, Macdonough's only path to the lake. Izard, now in command and resident at Plattsburgh, sent word to Macomb (whom he had ordered to Burlington) warning of the British fleet's movements. Macomb sent additional troops to Vergennes to man the battery at the mouth of the river.[23]

The British fleet moved on to anchor off Split Rock near the village of Essex on the New York shore of the lake. On Sunday the fourteenth, it moved across the lake to enter Otter Creek but was driven off by the fire from the American battery there. Macdonough reported to the secretary of the navy, "The battery, commanded by captain Thornton of the artillery, who was gallantly assisted by lieutenant Cassin of the Navy, received but little injury, although a number of shell were thrown, and many lodged in the parapet." There were two American injuries; neither serious. Troops were placed about the shoreline in the event that a British landing was attempted; none occurred. After an hour and a half, Pring turned to and sailed down the lake. Christie said of Pring's failed event: "Finding the enemy prepared for his reception, he judged it expedient to abandon his intended plan of attack." On the fifteenth, Macdonough did succeed in placing his fleet on the lake, unmolested.[24]

Eleazer Williams dined with generals Mooers and Woolsey, Judge Moores and Peter Sailly on the evening of the sixteenth. The evening's discussion was of the previous campaigns in the north. Meeting again on the eighteenth, the gentlemen generated what they believed to be the best plan of action for the Northern Army; Williams presented the plan in a document to General Izard. The general sought Williams during the following week to discuss the document the group had generated. Williams's journal reflects that the general seemed pleased with its suggestions.[25]

Aboard the *Saratoga*. *From Panel 3, City of Plattsburgh Heritage Trail. Lee Hunt, 1993. Used with permission.*

For the next week, British row galleys harassed the commercial steamboat on its trips to and from Plattsburgh and Burlington until the *Saratoga* began to sail the lake. Macdonough arrived at Plattsburgh on the twenty-sixth, announcing his presence with a salute from his ship's guns. He informed General Izard that the fleet, while short of the total complement of men, was ready for action.

Reporting to Secretary Jones, he wrote that the *Saratoga* sailed and worked well; likewise, the schooner and galleys. On the same day, British major general Frederick Robinson, who would play an important part in the coming months at Plattsburgh, left Lower Anglette in France for Bordeaux "to join the expedition there forming against some part of North America." On the twentieth, Bathurst issued secret orders for the movement of troops under the command of General Robert Ross who would create a "diversion on the Coast of the United States of America in favour [*sic*] of the Army employed in the defence [*sic*] of Upper & Lower Canada."[26]

Williams heard on June 3 that General Izard would deploy part of the army north, perhaps in response to reports that there was a significant effort to build a large ship at Isle aux Noix and that Pring's flotilla was on the lake some two miles below the border. The Halifax newspaper was reporting massive troop movements from Europe to the American continent.

Williams communicated his latest information to the War Department. The Plattsburgh paper reported that a light brigade (Fourth, Tenth and Twelfth Regiments of infantry, Colonel Forsythe's riflemen and two companies of light artillery) under the command of General Thomas Smith was now camped at the Dead Creek.

The reports from Halifax were correct; the press had scooped the occurrence. On June 3, Bathurst wrote in "secret" to Prevost informing him that thousands of troops and supplies would shortly arrive in Canada, and writing separately to General John Coape Sherbrooke, Bathurst ordered troops from Halifax to mount an attack "to occupy the part of Maine which at present intercepts the Communications between Halifax and Quebec." The actions foretold by Zebulon Pike a year earlier had begun. The new British arrivals, many of whom were veterans of the Peninsular War, would form the largest British force to assemble on the American continent during the war. In accordance with Bathurst's orders, Prevost was to use the force to invade the United States and gain control of Lake Champlain. To aid in the successful deployment of the plan, Bathurst had previously ordered a series of diversionary attacks on the coastline of the United States and the occupation of Maine. These were to be followed by "a more serious attack on some part of the Coasts of the United States"—this, perhaps, a veiled notice of the attacks on Washington and Baltimore. "These operations will not fail to effect a powerful diversion in your favor," he wrote. The orders urged an offensive against the United States that would result in "the entire destruction of Sackets Harbor and the Naval Establishments on Lake Erie and Lake Champlain." There was an emphasis on Lake Champlain and an urging, "If you deem it expedient expel the Enemy from it, and occupy it." Curiously, however, there was included a cautionary warning: "Always however taking care not to expose His Majesty's Forces to being cut off by too extended a line of advance." These contrasting objectives may have set the trap for Prevost's handling of what would be a defeat for Bathurst's plan.[27]

Macdonough reported the increased building activity of the British to Secretary Jones; the enemy had indeed laid the keel of a thirty-two-gun ship, a vessel larger than the *Saratoga*. He noted that the British were also receiving eleven galleys from Quebec. Again, Macdonough requested manpower in his letter on June 11. Captain Oliver H. Perry, in response to the request of Secretary Jones, transferred fifty-seven men to Lake Champlain and the command of Macdonough. Lieutenant Peter Gamble was ordered from the *Enterprise* to proceed to Lake Champlain. Macdonough was concerned that at Montreal, the frames of four vessels had been received, two of which were said to be destined for Lake Champlain. He told Jones that the enemy "intends risquing nothing, but will endeavour to out build us," and that from the protection of Isle aux Noix, the British would not engage him "until he feels himself strong enough to risk a battle." Macdonough suggested that if the building of additional vessels was felt to be necessary, they should be schooners or brigs, which would be more useful, in his opinion, than galleys—less manpower was required to navigate them, and the gun-carrying power was significantly enhanced. Macdonough vowed not to risk his vessels but would tease the enemy at the lines in an attempt to engage them on the open lake; he did so a few days later.[28]

On the twelfth, Smith's Light Brigade moved from Dead Creek to the lines in response to news of the arrival of one thousand men at LaColle. Eleazer Williams was made aware by communications from the commissary at French Mills and from Governor Tompkins that the government was considering discontinuing the distribution of rations to St. Regis. He immediately consulted with General Mooers and Peter Sailly and sent Commissary Hastings from French Mills to Albany to speak directly with the commissary general.[29]

By the middle of the month, more troops were evident at Plattsburgh; Colonel Pearce arrived with several hundred from the south. Dearborn was transferred to Boston, replaced by General Morgan Lewis. Williams's rangers reported serious preparations on behalf of the British, "The enemy is, no doubt, active in his preparation, either for the invasion or self-defence."[30]

From across the Atlantic, General Robinson would sail aboard the *York* with the departing British fleet. Ordered not to open their sealed orders until at sea, the sons of Britain would not be returning home just yet. The fleet made sail, the troops not knowing where they were being sent. Robinson recorded in his journal, "On the 16th the fleet sailed, all the Generals having sealed orders to be opened in a certain latitude…Upon opening our sealed orders, we found that the armament was destined for Quebec."[31]

On the nineteenth, Macdonough sought Jones's permission to build a brig or schooner with long eighteen-pounders to counter the enemy's galleys: "Her long guns would reach the gallies [*sic*] of the enemy, and in a breeze she would have a decided advantage over them." This request arrived just after Jones had told the secretary of war that Macdonough would build no more vessels for duty on Lake Champlain. Two days later, twenty additional sailors arrived for duty on the lake.[32]

Caleb Nichols from Crab Island corresponded directly with the secretary of war regarding his observations, analysis and opinion regarding the war in and around Plattsburgh. In short, he was a spy, an intelligence resource for the Department of War. He continued in that capacity throughout the summer. Nichols was in an interesting position to see the comings and goings on the lake and to receive news of movements from visitors. He sent a letter to the secretary of war on the twenty-third observing that "the Enemy Seem inclined to concentrate at the Stone Mill" and warned of the presence of "Ten Thousand of Lord Wellington's best European Troops."

Colonel Forsythe departed for the border with his riflemen and after crossing the border engaged a force near Odelltown. Upon discovering that the enemy force was about to close the route behind him from both sides, he ordered a return, crossing the border and stopping at the Hamilton house in Champlain. There, he ordered a stand against the advancing force. Two men were killed and one was wounded before the British withdrew.[33]

Macdonough again wrote to Jones on the twenty-sixth after hearing that the new vessel being built at Isle aux Noix could be expected on the lake by August. The new British vessel was built "having two gun decks in her

The British open fire. *Author's sketch.*

bow and stern, and mounting, among her guns, 28 long 24 pounders." He repeated his previous request to build an additional ship and supported it with his warning that he must remain at least equal to the British. "As the increase of our force will have to be so considerable," he wrote, he would have to build a vessel of the size "not less than an 18 gun brig." Perhaps to persuade the secretary into an immediate answer, Macdonough reminded Jones that sufficient lumber was available and that the Brown brothers could immediately begin to build the new ship at Vergennes.[34]

Smuggling continued to plague the American efforts. James Fisk of Barre, Vermont, writing to the secretary of war on the twenty-seventh of June, said, "Droves of cattle are continually passing from the northern parts of this state into Canada to the British." On the water, also, despite the considerable increase in the American fleet, supplies were floating north. Macdonough's navy intercepted and destroyed spars (one eighty feet; the other eighty-five feet) being towed north to be sold to the benefit of the British fleet. The citizen smugglers escaped. Perhaps to further support his building of the additional vessel, Fisk wrote again to Jones on the twenty-ninth: "It is supposed from the size of these spars that one was for the fore the other the mizzen mast," referring to the new British ship. "The main mast may also be on its way which we shall keep a good lookout for," he continued.[35]

Izard had learned that a force of over 5,000 had gathered just north of the border and that the obstructions placed in the roadways during the previous winter had been removed. Anticipating an invasion, he ordered that a fortification be built on Cumberland Head to house four eighteen-pounders looking out over the lake. Izard sent General Smith with 1,400 men north; Colonel Pearce was ordered to depart shortly thereafter with 800 men. Writing to the secretary of war to advise him of the current situation, Izard complained about the lack of horses and requested cannons, the poor-quality clothing received, and outlined his plan in the face of the new threat. He planned to leave a small force at Plattsburgh to man the fortification on Cumberland Head and take all available remaining forces north.

On the twenty-eighth, at the direction of General Smith, a small detachment of Forsythe's men again crossed the border in an attempt to engage part of the British force. They were to entice the British by withdrawing southward and all the while "keep up a retreating fire and endeavor to draw them into the ambuscade," a tactic advocated by Caleb Nichols in his letter to the secretary of war on the twenty-third. They succeeded in drawing the enemy over the line, where Forsythe and the remainder of his riflemen were waiting. Rather than leading the advancing British into Smith's larger force,

Forsythe stubbornly ordered his men to stand. In the midst of the fighting that resulted, Forsythe suffered a fatal wound near the collar bone and fell before the British withdrew; he died, the only American casualty, and was buried the next day at Champlain. Command of the rifle company devolved to the recent Plattsburgh arrival, Major Daniel Appling of the Rifle Corps. "Forsythe is Dead," Nichols wrote as he began his letter to Armstrong on the thirtieth. "He had too much Courage or too little prudence or rather cunning for the Rifle." In the same letter, Nichols urged the immediate reinforcement of the Northern Army with rifle companies "and the most expert woodsmen" to draw the British off the roadways and into the woods, where the advantage would be with the American riflemen.[36]

The spring of 1814 brought the blossoming of flora in the north and a burgeoning British presence close to Plattsburgh, the withering of a faulty American military plan and the initiation of a masterfully crafted British plan.

5
Posture and Preparation
(July/August 1814)

A gain, in the beginning of July, the secretary of the navy reinforced his decision that Macdonough would not be permitted to add to his fleet on Lake Champlain. The secretary of war immediately wrote to General Izard. He told Izard of the discussions at a meeting on the second and concluded, "We are, therefore, driven to the expedient of fortifying the narrows." The prophetic letter continued:

> The late events in Europe give to the enemy a great disposable force, and the means, of course, of being very formidable. The newspapers report, that large armaments are to be sent hither; but of the actual sailing of these, we have no advice. The next arrivals from Europe will show whether the story be merely made up to operate on the negotiation, or is the precursor of a new and increased activity on the part of the enemy in prosecuting the war.[1]

Izard followed the directions given and added to the fortifications that he had already started. For the works south of the village, he proposed, "A few redoubts, judiciously placed, and flanking each other, will enable a small force to resist numbers for a given time, and will render the favourite mode of proceeding of the enemy in destroying public buildings and depots, more difficult than heretofore." He approved of the recent policy of offering a reward for information regarding deserters but spoke of an "alarming" increase in desertions among troops en route to Plattsburgh. He spoke of the recent arrival of a detachment from Greenbush "of about one hundred and sixty men, twenty-six deserted on the road."

Regiments arriving at Plattsburgh included a number of black soldiers, a trend noted by Altoff as being prevalent in the operations of the northern army in 1813 and 1814. Izard sought the secretary's counsel in dealing with the recent arrival of "negroes and people of colour" among the New England regiments sent to Plattsburgh. When their country—our country—asked for assistance in its defense, many enlisted in the military. John Alfred of Vermont; John Bowen of North Hampton, Massachusetts; Jacob Palmer of New London, Connecticut; Samuel Stanley of Oxford Massachusetts; Francis Thompson of Bethlehem, New York; Cato Williams of Lanesborough, Massachusetts; and many other farmers left their homes and families, eventually serving at Plattsburgh.

Farming was not the only livelihood of black Americans, and the enlisted ranks of the military reflected the diversity of occupations of the time: William Sherbourne from Londonderry, New Hampshire, was a mariner before enlisting; Peter Simpson from Brookfield, Connecticut, a shoemaker; Joseph Weldell of Boston, a rope maker; John Brown of Huntington, New York, a blacksmith; John Moore of Danbury, Connecticut, a laborer; and James Gomaus, a baker. They all served at Plattsburgh.

Izard's officers refused to work with the "negroes and people of colour"; these soldiers were formed into a pioneer corps (essentially, a labor gang). "Shall they be retained and mustered in that capacity?" Izard asked the secretary. No direct answer to his question has been found. These patriots were given the task of building fortifications.[2]

Amid the preparations for war, the army and the community took time to celebrate the anniversary of the country's independence. Eleazer Williams tells of a "festival day" in the dining company of Captain Sperry and Mr. Sailly. While the Americans celebrated, the British Third, Fifth, Twenty-seventh and Fifty-eighth Regiments under the command of Major General Power left Bordeaux in ships bound for Canada.[3]

On the fifth, a relenting Jones ordered John Bullus, the New York naval agent, to contract with Noah Brown for the immediate building of an eighteen-gun brig for use on Lake Champlain. He did not communicate his decision to Macdonough, who again wrote to the secretary on the ninth, and yet again on the thirteenth, arguing for an additional vessel.

The Brown brothers, Noah and Adam, came to Lake Champlain and used materials that were immediately available. From the yard in Vergennes, Vermont, they combed the forests for white oak—the strong, durable material that grew in abundance in the region. Oak was the logical and best choice for the shipwrights. Recent archaeological findings confirm its use. Materials examined from the discovered hulks of the *Ticonderoga* and *Eagle* show a preponderance of white oak. The *Ticonderoga*'s external oak planking averaged three inches thick; the *Eagle*'s, two inches. Oak planks in thicker dimensions were used beneath the gun ports and in other critical structural areas. Pine was used within the vessels for the ceilings (floor planking); other native woods (maple, elm, ash, chestnut) were used throughout the vessels' interiors.

More good news arrived for Macdonough as Sailing Master Loomis, who had commanded the previously captured *Eagle*, was released by the British and reported for duty at Plattsburgh.[4]

The local paper of the ninth included the following curious information: "Lieut. Mix, of the Navy, the Torpedo Man, has joined the fleet on Lake Champlain." Lieutenant Mix was a member of the Torpedo Service, a new and mostly experimental group who utilized underwater mines in the attempt to destroy British ships. The method of warfare was termed barbaric by the British and was the subject of some discussion in British periodicals. There was never a successful mining of a British ship in the war. It may be that the art of suggestion was employed in an attempt to deceive, as there is no evidence to suggest that Lieutenant Mix ever arrived at Plattsburgh. No indication has been found that the British were dissuaded in their future plans toward Plattsburgh by hearing of the supposed presence of Lieutenant Mix.[5]

Eleazer Williams headed for the border to gain fresh information of the British. He learned that they were expecting reinforcements from Europe. Writing in his journal of the expected arrival of part of Wellington's veterans, he thought the American forces capable of meeting them. Caleb Nichols also learned of the British diversionary plan to attack the eastern coast while advancing from the north. He gathered this intelligence from Dr. Woods, then living on the lakeshore. Woods had been asked to transport British General Baynes to a meeting with American Colonel Lear at Dewey's Tavern in Champlain. The general told the doctor of Admiral Cochrane's fleet off the eastern coast in the Atlantic and the plan to "enter all the harbors and destroy all the public property and defences in them." Nichols warned, "It may be the intention of the Enemy to attack our Coast for the purpose of drawing our Troops from this quarter or to prevent them being Sent here."[6]

To the south, the British navy entered the Potomac and was reported to have landed 1,500 troops near Washington; locally, the naval building activity about Lake Champlain increased at fever pitch. John Bullus, the naval agent, informed Macdonough of shipments of hawsers (heavy mooring rope), rigging and cordage for the new American brig. On the lake, Macdonough's sailors destroyed another four spars headed for the border.

For the new American ship, Macdonough contemplated the name *Eagle* and requested a complement of guns and officers: two lieutenants, a sailing master, a surgeon and a master commandant.[7]

Eleazer Williams continued to gain information regarding activity near the border. He interrogated a spy on the twenty-third who contributed the names of Americans who were working favorably with the British. He also learned the names of Canadian citizens acting as secret agents near the border in Canada. Williams's rangers were instructed to follow the movements of each of them, seizing the Canadians if they crossed the border.[8]

Again, just weeks after capturing and destroying spars made in the United States and headed for the British forces in Canada, Macdonough's navy seized a raft made from about thirteen thousand board feet of plank and oak spars on which twenty-seven barrels of tar were being floated north.

On the twenty-fifth, Macdonough sought Eleazer Williams's help in gaining information on the state of the new British vessel at Isle aux Noix. Williams had just learned that troops had arrived at Quebec from Europe. The Third Regiment (Buffs) sent word from the transport *Barton* to the military secretary, Captain Noah Freer, that they had, that day, anchored off Quebec with 12 officers and 222 men. The Buffs were ordered to "proceed to Montreal, leaving their sick women at Quebec." Four days later, the Fifth, Twenty-seventh and Fifty-eighth Regiments and a detachment of the Royal Artillery arrived.[9]

Border skirmishes were becoming more frequent, and on the twenty-seventh, the Plattsburgh paper contained an account of such a case:

> *On Thursday morning last, captain Nelson, of the 10ᵗʰ Infantry, with a small detachment surprised the British picket at Smith's, in Odelltown, killed a Lieut. Made nine prisoners, and put the rest to flight. The prisoners, (a sergt. maj. qr. mas. sergt. 2 sergts. & 5 privates) were brought to this place yesterday morning—The enemy's Indians are constantly hovering about the lines.*

Caleb Nichols was now convinced of the urgency of the situation at Plattsburgh and warned Armstrong, "Its at length developed that the Enemy has never had so great a force on or near this frontier." His letter passed details of the new British ship being built, its state of completion and the fact that it would be equipped with a furnace. He cautioned that the American navy on Lake Champlain might be nothing more than "fuel to be lighted by the British floating battery."[10]

Posture and Preparation (July/August 1814)

A small detachment of American dragoons and 50 men of the Fifteenth Regiment arrived at Plattsburgh during the last week of the month. Within days, General Macomb departed from Plattsburgh with the Sixth, Thirteenth, Fifteenth, Sixteenth and Twenty-ninth Regiments in bateaux for Chazy Landing—a force of 1,100—leaving only his sick and wounded.

In a letter to the secretary of war on the last day of the month, Izard enclosed a Quebec handbill that touted the arrival of several thousand troops from Europe. He expressed his disappointment with his fellow countrymen who were supplying the British, his frustration with the army for not paying the men on a regular basis and the slow arrival of reinforcements. He continued:

> *From the St. Lawrence to the ocean, an open disregard prevails for the laws prohibiting intercourse with the enemy. The road to St. Regis is covered with droves of cattle, and the river with rafts, destined for the enemy...On the eastern side of lake Champlain, the high roads are found insufficient for the supplies of cattle which are pouring into Canada. Like herds of buffaloes, they press through the forest, making paths for themselves...Were it not for these supplies, the British forces in Canada would soon be suffering from famine, or their government be subjected to enormous expense for their maintenance.*

General Daniel Bissell would take the Fifth, Fourteenth, Thirtieth, Thirty-first, Thirty-third, Thirty-fourth and Forty-fifth Regiments north on the same day, completing Izard's 4,500-man force on the move to Sackets Harbor.

At Plattsburgh, Major Joseph Totten of the engineers was left to complete the fortifications with "two incomplete companies of artillery, all the sick, and a working party [pioneers], of between three and four hundred men, here, under command of Colonel Fenwick." Access to the fortifications was to be preceded by trenches of sufficient depth and width to foul any escalade (scaling of the walls). Any ladder that the British might use in attempting to cross the trench would have to be in excess of twenty feet long. The twelve-foot wide, eight-foot-deep trench sides were angled steeply upward on the fortifications' sides, forming ramparts of sixteen feet topped by two-foot parapets. The trenches were fraised—the angled, sharpened stakes imbedded in the trench bottom so as to present a thorny welcome for any raiding party. In addition, the bastions (blockhouse-style boxes at the corners of the fortification) projected far enough that the trenches beside them were within the view and range of any weapon used within them. In short, the

American trench formed a serious obstruction and offered no cover for an advancing force.[11]

From across the border on August 1, a raiding party of British soldiers and Indians entered Champlain, attacking the northern picket guard; four American soldiers were wounded. Reinforcements continued to arrive. Two days later, another battalion of infantry under a Major Sizer reported for duty at Plattsburgh. On Thursday, the fourth, an apprehensive Peter Sailly wrote to the superintendent of public supplies, speaking of the reports from Canadian newspapers of eleven regiments of the "army of Wellington" arriving at Quebec. He felt that an attack was imminent and reported that military equipment from Plattsburgh had been sent to Whitehall.[12]

On August 3, the day when the Royal Hampshire Regiment arrived at Quebec from Europe, Eleazer Williams reported to Commodore Macdonough, as he had been requested to do, on the progress of the British warship being built at Isle aux Noix. The enemy had succeeded in gaining all the spars for the new ship, and it was near completion. The Royal Hampshires were detailed to Kingston. The intent of the British was in keeping with the orders previously given to General Prevost: threaten an attack at Sackets Harbor to draw the American forces away from Plattsburgh, the ultimate prize.[13]

The British general Frederick Philipse Robinson's journal notes that his regiments arrived in Quebec on the ninth. The Third Brigade of the Left Division now included "Royal Artillery, 207; 3rd Foot, 851; 27th, 1010; Royal Artillery Horses, 184; 5th Foot, 940; 58th, 793." With the movement of troops to Kingston, the threat was initiated, and the stage was set. An army of approximately fourteen thousand sat near Montreal, an army that included a large percentage of Britain's seasoned veteran troops. A quarter of Britain's peninsular infantry had been sent to North America along with a number of artillery companies.

Eleazer Williams wrote in his journal of the apparent British ruse at Sackets Harbor and that Izard had been ordered to move against it. Astonished, Williams wrote, "This will be another blunder of the present administration." The frustrated General Izard immediately wrote to the secretary of war.[14]

Macdonough reported to Secretary Jones on the same day. The work of planking the new American brig had begun, and the vessel would be launched on the fifteenth—without officers, he reminded the secretary. He formally asked that the vessel be named *Eagle*.[15]

On the tenth, the secretary of war wrote to General Izard of his previous correspondence regarding a move toward the west. The secretary questioned, "Will it not be advisable to strengthen the several posts on lake Champlain, by military detachments?" and authorized the general to "call on the governors of New York, and Vermont, for this species of troops" if he thought it necessary. The secretary clearly did not comprehend the gravity of the situation that existed on the northern front. The records of the British Buffs address the movement of "a brigade under Sir James Kempt to make a diversion on the eastern shores of Lake Ontario and thus draw off a portion of the American force from his own front." Worse, Izard had not received the secretary's previous letter. Izard continued planning for the secretary's "project," as he had been directed. Contacting Captain Chauncy on Lake Ontario, Izard sought to arrange for naval transportation of his force from Ogdensburg into Canada. If he would attack, he would do so from the north. Izard replied to the letter that he had last received from the secretary, enclosing a "statement of the arrivals at Quebec, from the 26th July to the 2[d] of August." His tone was respectful but direct and forceful:

> *I will make the movement you direct, if possible; but I shall do it with the apprehension of risking the force under my command, and with the certainty that every thing in this vicinity, but the lately erected works at Plattsburg and Cumberland Head, will, in less than three days after my departure, be in the possession of the enemy. He is in force superior to mine in my front; he daily threatens an attack on my position at Champlain; we are all in hourly expectation of a serious conflict. That he has not attacked us before this time, is attributable to caution on his part, from exaggerated reports of our numbers, and from his expectation of reinforcements. You will ask why I have changed my view of this subject since my letter of the 19th July? On that day, I knew of the proceedings at the westward no more than you had communicated in the plan of the campaign, forwarded by Colonel Snelling, and than I had read in the newspapers. The second division was advancing. I had not advanced, with the whole of my disposable force, to the frontier line; nor had I certain information of what was in my front; nor did I forsee that neither men, nor funds for the Quartermaster's department, would arrive. Let me not be supposed to hesitate about executing any project, which the government I have the honour to serve think proper to direct. My little army will do its duty. I only desire to have the difficulties which I have to contend with, properly understood. It has always been my conviction, that the numerical force of the enemy has been underrated. I believe this to be the strong point of our frontier, for either attack or defence; and I know that a British force has been kept in check in Lower Canada, for many*

weeks past, greatly superior to that which I could oppose to it. These things I mention, sir, because although I anticipate disappointment, I will guard myself against disgrace.[16]

Macdonough's new brig was launched on the twelfth, without the necessary complement of officers and crew. From what he knew, the new British ship would be ready by September 1. Macdonough approached a reluctant General Izard requesting assistance with manning; for lack of navy personnel, army troops would be aboard the new brig. Again, Macdonough wrote to Secretary Jones:

Can Master Commandant Creighton be spared from the sea board to command this Brig? All my officers are young and many of them inexperienced. The recruiting service is dull and I am advised of but fifteen men being entered for the Brig although three rendezvous are opened for her—one at New York, one at Newport and its vicinity and Commodore Bainbridge has ordered one to be opened in Boston. The Brig will be ready to enter the lake before she gets her crew unless a transfer of men could be made from some vessel or station on the sea board…The enemy has collected in considerable numbers at the line near the lake and threaten an attack both by land and water.[17]

The impact of the British feint at Sackets Harbor and westward began to have the desired effect. General Armstrong ordered that provisions from Plattsburgh be forwarded to the west. Eleazer Williams received word from the governor that the army at Plattsburgh would also be moved to meet the apparent threat to the west, a move he termed "a most extraordinary step in the military policy." His journal carries the thought of the results of the move: an invasion was possible once Plattsburgh was unprotected by any significant force. He wrote:

Now, this is most impolitic, as well as contrary to the military tactics, to leave such an important post as Plattsburg, just at this time, where the government has everything here to sustain the campaign. Artillery of various calibre, abundance of munition of war, provisions and arms for ten thousand men, 700 bateaux complete for use, and a navy ready for action. I am somewhat disheartened with the manoeuvres, and errors of the government. Commodore Macdonough is greatly chagrined at the intentions of the government in regard to this matter.

It is important to remember that Armstrong had been warned in July through the careful analysis of Eleazer Williams, the Native American spy, and Caleb Nichols, the American spy/resident of Crab Island, of the strong British force to the north and the apparent object of the British invasion plan: Plattsburgh.[18]

At St. Johns, the British were gathering every wagon that could be used to transport supplies for the move south. At Plattsburgh, Captain Woolsey gathered the Veteran Exempts to help in the preparations for a defense; they would assist in the preparation of the fortifications. The final orders were received by General Izard from Armstrong: the move west would proceed immediately. The next day, an astonished Williams wrote to the War Department through Governor Tompkins, warning of the impending danger to the north. Williams learned of the movements of British troops to La Prairie and L'Acadia plains, assembling for an invasion south. At Plattsburgh, the talk of a large massing of British to the north must have been reinforced by the sounds coming from that direction. The British General Robinson, now commanding the brigade at Chamblee, ordered practice firings and the training of the light companies "in skirmishing in woods, after the American fashion." A complement of 182 Royal marines was ordered to the British ships of Lake Champlain.[19]

Again on August 17, Nichols warned Armstrong of the impending invasion: "The British are I believe concentrating all of their Forces, as they arrive, in Odelltown and as soon as they are ready I've no doubt intend by Superior numbers to force their way to Plattsburgh to capture the U.S. Army…If this Position is once lost we may never look forward to the time in which we can coerce Great Britain to Peace."

While the *Eagle* was launched and due to arrive at Plattsburgh on the twentieth, there were insufficient men to crew it. Macdonough expressed his concerns again to Secretary Jones. The officers had not arrived, and with Izard given orders to march west, the forty men whom Macdonough had hoped for would not be detailed from Izard's force to assist the navy. Macdonough hoped that the enemy's ship, soon to be launched, would not be ready for service until sometime in September. His concerns were set aside a few days later when he learned that Lieutenant Robert Henley and fifty-two crew members had arrived at Vergennes and, lacking only sails, would be at Plattsburgh soon. The British gunboats were now adventuring farther south on a daily basis, coming as far as Point au Fer (off Champlain) to fire their guns in annoyance.[20]

Izard, in accordance with his orders, made preparations to move his forces. To the secretary of war, he again expressed his objection with the plan and, warning of the consequences, reported anew the strength of the force to his north: "I must not be responsible for the consequences of abandoning my present strong position. I will obey orders, and execute them as well as I know how. Major General Brisbane commands at Odelltown, he is said to have between five and six thousand men with him. At Chambly are stated to be about four thousand." Izard would leave General Macomb in charge of the remaining 1,500 troops at Plattsburgh. Eleazer Williams tells of his meeting with Macomb on the nineteenth and his confusion at the general's first thoughts that the British, massing to the north, might also move west.[21]

On the twenty-first, the *Eagle* started down Otter Creek from Vergennes. After several days loading supplies and completing the remaining tasks necessary for its completion, the *Eagle* entered the lake on the twenty-sixth and, traveling down the lake with all sails set, arrived at Plattsburgh on the twenty-seventh.[22]

General Izard sent another lengthy letter to the secretary of war on the twenty-third in which he detailed the results of a council of war that he held to discuss the route the troops would take to Sackets Harbor. With the long train of troops and baggage that would be necessary, the risks of taking the northern route through Chateaugay and Ogdensburg would be an enemy attack and a severing of the line. Instead, they chose a southern route through Lake George and Schenectady. Izard would depart without artillery, leaving all the "sick and convalescents, and about 1,200 effectives" behind. His division consisted of "dragoons, light artillery (armed as infantry), the 4th, 5th, 10th, 12th, 13th, 14th, 15th, 16th, and 45th infantry (making a total of about four thousand effectives)." In accordance with the secretary's orders, Izard ordered General Mooers to call out the militia, one regiment of infantry and one troop of light dragoons.[23]

In the afternoon of the same day, General Macomb asked for Eleazer Williams's rangers to provide frequent reports on the British activities at La Prairie and L'Acadia plains. He ordered "the whole garrison to labor upon the forts for their completion." The following day, after meeting with Macomb and Macdonough, Williams left for the northern line accompanied by a naval officer in civilian dress. He received reports from his rangers that confirmed the size of the British force and that it was, indeed, headed for Plattsburgh. The militia began to assemble. General Macomb, upon hearing of the latest reports, would hold a council of war on the twenty-sixth, which General Mooers would attend. As the village began to empty of its citizens, the military officers discussed the defense of Plattsburgh against an enemy of superior numbers. In addition to the New

York militia, a request would be made to the State of Vermont for militia assistance and for such citizens who would remain to help with the forts. Williams wrote in his journal of the citizen migration in the face of the coming event: "It is not only melancholy, but distressing, to see the poor taking their all upon their backs, and flying from their peaceful abodes, and seeking an asylum in places where they are unknown."

On the same day, British General Baynes wrote a secret communiqué to Lieutenant General Drummond informing him of the movement of the Thirty-seventh Regiment toward Kingston and their plan to attack or effect a siege of Sackets Harbor; the British army entered and burned Washington—Bathurst's plan had been implemented in full. The British government waited only for the news that the feint at Sackets Harbor had been effective in convincing the United States War Department to draw strength away from Plattsburgh, the ultimate prize.[24]

On August 27, Izard officially turned over command of Plattsburgh to Macomb. Izard reminded Macomb that cooperation with Macdonough would be necessary and that if Plattsburgh was attacked, "I anticipate much distinction for the commandant and credit for the troops." Major Totten and Lieutenant Trescott of the Engineers would remain behind to attend to the completion of the forts; Captain Sproull of the Thirteenth Regiment would take charge of any detachments of infantry Macomb could raise. General Mooers had not yet called out the New York infantry or dragoons as requested on the twenty-third, apparently feeling that he did not have the authority. Izard addressed the issue to the governor.[25]

Macomb, now in charge, set all hands to work and asked Eleazer Williams for a report of the British movements every ten hours. Macomb would describe his charges to his father: "Our whole force does not exceed 1,500 effectives…My troops are the remnant of Gen. Izard's Army, invalids and convalescents, except about 600 men." Amidst the building of the batteries, Williams sought Macomb to deliver a 4:00 p.m. report. The surprised Williams found the general working among his troops, carrying logs, so covered with dirt that Williams almost overlooked him. Caleb Nichols wrote of the "confusion and distress" of the situation at Plattsburgh: "I am not a judge, but I should Suppose the Small force left here by Gen. Izard, notwithstanding our fortifications, will fall into the hands of the Enemy."[26]

Macdonough requested information from Williams regarding the enemy fleet's guns. The new British ship's gun complement would fit out at over thirty, bringing their total to ninety-four. Macdonough was pleased with the report Williams's men had been able to provide. The American fleet, with ninety-two guns now available, was near parity in metal, but Macdonough had not seen his full complement of sailors and officers.

The British naval manning situation was not much better than Macdonough's. Commodore Yeo yanked Captain Fisher from the *Confiance* project, replacing him with Captain Downie, who had returned from Lake Ontario. Captain Pring of the Royal Navy would later write of the same disappointing day and the *Confiance* having "an unorganized Crew, comprised of several Drafts of Men; who had recently arrived from different ships at Quebec, many of whom only joined the day before, and were totally unknown either to the Officers or to each other." Pushing the schedule, Prevost ordered that the quartermaster suspend all tasks that would interfere with the procurement of fittings and equipment for the new ship.

With Lieutenant Henley and the new brig *Eagle* on station at Plattsburgh, he and his crew were set to work receiving and distributing supplies and quickly preparing the vessel "for service." Again, Macdonough wrote to the secretary of war to inform him of the latest reports and the unresolved manning shortage.[27]

Williams reported on the twenty-eighth: "Fourteen thousand regulars, most of whom were lately from Europe; two thousand Canadians and two hundred Indians; thirty-six guns, and about one thousand carts. Three thousand of the above troops were thirty-six miles above Montreal, on their way into the Upper province. When the news reached Montreal that General Izard had left Plattsburg with his army (excepting a heavy guard), on his way to the west, they were recalled." Williams's diary entry speaks of the British being so confident that they "declare[d] openly that Plattsburgh was their object."[28]

The British began their advance toward the border on the twenty-ninth as Izard was leaving with the last regiment from Plattsburgh. Izard dallied as long as he could in expectation of word from the War Department to recall his force. The advance that the British General Robinson later termed a "secret expedition" had begun. In light of the newspaper accounts of troop movements and the confident open declarations Williams's rangers reported, the mission was hardly secret. It's hard to hide a fourteen-thousand-man army. Along with those of Generals Power and Brisbane, Robinson moved his force south on the thirtieth. Brisbane moved into United States territory, stopping at Champlain. Power was behind at Burtonville, and Robinson's brigade would stop at L'Acadia. Brisbane issued a general order to the brigade directing that all soldiers were to conduct themselves in the highest manner of gentlemanly decorum:

"A British Light Infantryman." John J. Purdy, 2008. *Author's private collection.*

> *That their conduct shall not bring disgrace on the British Army…for the inhabitants of the country, finding they are properly treated and protected, will bring every article necessary into the camps; for those who remain quiet in their* [homes] *not in the smallest degree to be molested, nor their property taken from them without their full* [approval], *and its being* [paid] *for, as it is not against such persons that Great Britain makes war.*

General Ross wrote to Bathurst of the successful Chesapeake campaign and the burning of Washington:

> *I have the honour to Communicate to your Lordship that on the night of the 24th Instant after Defeating the Army of the United States on that day the Troops under my Command entered and took possession of the City of Washington—In compliance with Your Lordships Instructions to*

attract the attention of the Government of the United States and to cause a Diversion in favour of the Army in Canada...

General Mooers finally called for the militia of Clinton and Essex Counties; the Plattsburgh militia was to be led by Lieutenant Colonel Miller.[29]

Macdonough had just transferred Second Lieutenant Joseph Smith from the *Saratoga* to the position of first lieutenant of the *Eagle*. He arrived with forty men from the *Saratoga* to man the guns. Lieutenant Henley, with the *Eagle* now fully rigged but marginally manned, set full sail from Plattsburgh for the north at four o'clock in the afternoon with the rest of the fleet. An hour later, the wind deadened, and the ships had to be towed by the row galleys. Macdonough eventually anchored the fleet off the southwest end of Isle La Motte, just north of Beekmantown and off Chazy.[30]

August ended with an uneasy air of anticipation. The question was not if, but when the British would descend on Plattsburgh. Those civilians who were left in Plattsburgh and the surrounding countryside took the best of their belongings and went south toward the Quaker Union and beyond, leaving their homes for the unknown.

6
Prelude to Battle
(September 1–10, 1814)

T he new British ship, *Confiance*, was nearing completion. On September 1, the newly assigned commander, George Downie, wrote requesting cannon locks (the firing devices that operate similar to the flintlock of a musket) from the ordnance storekeeper at Quebec. His sense of urgency regarding the *Confiance* and the performance of its guns was quite blunt: "In a few days she will be before the Enemy, & the want of locks may be seriously injurious in the Action."[1]

In Plattsburgh, Macdonough and Macomb had been receiving regular reports of the British troop movements across the border and their fleet preparations. They decided that the best defense would be effected by moving Macdonough's fleet back to Plattsburgh, into Cumberland Bay. In the early afternoon, with only a light wind, Macdonough ordered the galleys to begin towing the larger vessels up the lake toward Plattsburgh. By three o'clock in the afternoon, the winds had returned, and in the dangerous task of setting sail aloft, Seaman James Willis of the *Eagle* fell to the deck and died shortly thereafter. The fleet anchored in the bay at Plattsburgh at nine o'clock. Macdonough advised Secretary Jones of the situation and the defensive decisions.[2]

As British General Robinson noted the difficulty of moving his brigades over the primitive roads toward the south, roads only made worse by the heavy-wheeled vehicles transporting the artillery and baggage, Lieutenant Colonel Miller's small Clinton County militia force advanced near the village of Chazy. In Plattsburgh, Macomb made his initial assignments for the rising defenses of the village south of the Saranac River. Major Vinson would command at what would be named Fort Scott, overlooking the bay;

Lieutenant Colonel Storrs at the fort on the Saranac (soon to be Fort Brown); and Colonel Melancton Smith, at the major fortification, Fort Moreau, between them. The blockhouse just north of the fortifications would be defended by Captain Smyth and the "convalescents," while a detachment of artillery under Lieutenant Fowler would be sent to the north blockhouse on the point at the mouth of the Saranac. Macdonough sent the sick of his fleet to the hospital and acknowledged the arrival of several sailors and officers.[3]

By the third, the British First Brigade was encamped at Champlain in huts built during the previous winter for the American forces. The Third Buffs occupied the store belonging to Pliney Moore, using it as a guardhouse. Moore would later file claims for damages to the store and his fences. A seventy-man detachment of the Thirty-eighth Light Regiment remained in Champlain as the major force moved south. Six British gunboats moved up the lake and anchored off the northern end of Isle La Motte. Macdonough expressed his thoughts to Secretary Jones that the British army would not advance farther south until its fleet was ready to sail; then it would attack by land and water. Eleazer Williams wrote of General Mooers's gathering militia "assembling, and forming an encampment in the rear of the forts and at Salmon River."

In the village, a group of boys from the Plattsburgh Academy, perhaps more normally seen playing "Saddle My Nag" or "Follow My Leader," witnessed their families preparing to move from the village, the reality of the advancing British army a looming threat. Denied their homes, possessions and familiarities, and possessing the impetuosity of youth, the boys vowed to fight. These were boys who had been taught to use muskets from an early age. Hunting for game to supplement the normal diet of the day was a common practice, and most boys were able with a weapon. Squirrels, rabbits and all manner of small game would have been the customary targets, but the thought of a British soldier in a red coat whose chest bore a large white "X" of crossed belts—imagine their thoughts! They approached General Macomb, who, while needing every gun, would agree only if they found military sponsors. Captain Martin Aikin of the Essex County militia and Lieutenant Azariah C. Flagg of the Clinton County militia (then editor of the *Plattsburgh Republican*) agreed. Aikin's Rifle Company, as they would be known, would play an important role in the days to come. As the boys were not of age for enlistment, their names do not appear on the daily muster rolls—only those of their officers, Aikin and Flagg. There were more than the fifteen whose names are normally seen; one, Peters, is known to have been killed on September 6. There were as many as twenty, not all remaining with the unit until the eleventh.[4]

Prelude to Battle (September 1–10, 1814)

American soldiers board Macdonough's fleet in Plattsburgh Bay, September 11, 1814. *From Panel 3, City of Plattsburgh Heritage Trail. Lee Hunt, 1993. Used with permission.*

In response to Macdonough's request for men, Macomb ordered 250 infantrymen to board Macdonough's ships as acting marines. Macomb's report of troop strength was passed by J.M. O'Connor, assistant adjutant general at Lake George, to General Izard:

> *Return and estimate of the forces left at Plattsburg (and its dependencies) on the 28ᵗʰ August, commanded by Brigadier General Alexander Macomb.*
>
> | | |
> |---|---:|
> | *For Duty Aggregate Detachments of the regiments and corps that marched* | *77* |
> | *Captain Leonard's company of Light Artillery* | *100* |
> | *Captain M'Glassin's, 15ᵗʰ Infantry* | *50* |
> | *6ᵗʰ, 29ᵗʰ, 30ᵗʰ, 31ˢᵗ, 33ᵈ, and 34ᵗʰ regts. of Infantry, reported from the aggregate present on the 31ˢᵗ of July 1771 Capt. Shell's company, 6ᵗʰ regt., arrived 9ᵗʰ Sept., (100 aggregate)* | *say 80* |
> | *Detachment of 13ᵗʰ regt. under Capt. Sproull,* | *estimated 200* |
>
> *For Duty 2,278*

79

Sick and Invalids of the Light Artillery and Dragoons,
the 4th, 5th, 10th, 12th, 14th, 15th, 16th, and 45th regts.
of Infantry, from regimental returns, for August, of
these regiments   *803*
On board the fleet, detachments from the infantry of
the line   *250*

Grand Aggregate 3,331

Of which force, it is presumed, that not more than one thousand are invalids and non-combatants. This return and estimate is believed to be under the total amount of forces left by a few hundreds; for instance, the 29th regiment was reinforced in August by a detachment under Major Sizer—and this regt. is reported from July.

   Omitted in the above—two veteran companies of the corps of Artillery commanded by Captain Alexander Brooks, U.S. Artillery.[5]

(Note: The "for duty" total adds up to 507. The grand aggregate, with sick, invalids and fleet detachments, then, numbers 1,560 and corresponds almost directly to the language of the previously mentioned Macomb letter to his father: "My troops are the remnant of Gen. Izard's Army, invalids and convalescents, except about 600 men.")

By the fourth, British General Robinson had moved his army south as far as Chazy; only the boldest of American militia ventured to engage them there. As mentioned, Robinson left the seventy-man Thirty-ninth Light Company at Chazy as he marched farther into the American countryside. The Second and Third Brigades would be ordered to rise before sunset and be armed, inspected and ready to march three miles south the next morning. Captain Pring, commanding the gunboats anchored off Isle La Motte, ordered that a battery be constructed for three long eighteen-pounders. The battery was to support the troops left at the Chazy River with the growing stockpile of supplies being deposited there.[6]

In Plattsburgh, militia forces from Vermont and the three New York counties of Clinton, Essex and Franklin were massing. The numbers of the combined New York militia amounted to only seven hundred. From Vermont, volunteers under General Strong were streaming into the encampments south of the forts. Macomb deployed an "advance guard" north and west of the village. He sent "Capt. Safford and Lieut. M.M. Standish with a troop of New York State cavalry" to the northwest and a rifle corps under

Prelude to Battle (September 1–10, 1814)

Lieutenant Appling and "Capt. Sproul, with two cannon and 200 American soldiers" to the Dead Creek bridge. In the wind and the rain of the fourth, the Americans cut trees to block the roadways north of the village along the lake route. Later, as they fell back toward the village, Sproul's men would remove planking from the bridge crossing the Dead Creek. These actions were taken in the hope of slowing the coming advance of the British columns; they would prove to be little more than an annoyance for the red-coated invaders. Aikin's young volunteers moved closer to the lines and stopped at West Chazy. After a council of war in the evening, and hearing of the latest movements of the enemy from Eleazer Williams, Macomb and his officers assumed that the British would approach Plattsburgh from both the lake road and the back road, through Beekmantown. Williams sent a small detachment under the command of his brother John into the night to establish a watch on the enemy encampment.[7]

The British advanced to the southern limits of Chazy on the fifth. They had easily overcome the felled trees and dismantled bridges before them. Prevost would later write to Bathurst of his success in the feint at Sackets Harbor: "As the Troops concentrated and approached the line of separation between this Province & the United States, the American Army abandoned its entrenched Camp on the River Chazy at Champlain, a position I immediately seized and occupied in force on the 31st inst." On the fifth, he said, "the whole of the left Division advanced to the Village of Chazy without meeting the least opposition from the Enemy." Macomb issued the following orders:

> *The General is now satisfied that the enemy will attack the post in a few days. He relies with confidence on the valor and intrepidity of those he has the honor to command. Let it not be said that Erie was better defended than Plattsburgh. It was there that the American Soldiers beat and defeated the heroes of Spain, France and Portugal, and their example must be followed or our reputation is lost. The eyes of America are on us and fortune always favors the brave. The works being now capable of resisting a powerful attack, the manner of defending them the General thinks it his duty to detail, that every man may know and do his duty. The troops will line the Parapet in two ranks, leaving intervals for the artillery. A reserve of one sixth of the whole force in Infantry will be detailed and paraded fronting the several angles of the works, which it will be their particular duty to sustain. To each bastion are to be assigned by the several commandants of the Forts a sufficient number of Infty to line all the faces in single rank of each line. Should the enemy gain the Ditch, the front rank of the Part assaulted*

will mount the Parrapet and repel him with its fire and the Bayonet. If the men of this rank are determined, no human force can Dispossess them of that position. The officers are commanded to put to instant death any man who deserts his Post. The principal work, Fort Moreau, is entrusted to the command of Col. Smyth, of the 29th Regt Infantry, having for its garrison the old 6th and his own Regt. The Redoubt No. [1] is entrusted to Lt. Col. Stores, and the detachments of the 30th and 31st will form its Garrison. Redoubt No. [2] is entrusted to Major Vinson and has for its garrison the 33d and 34. The Block house near Platt's is entrusted to captain Smyth 1st Rifle Regt and has for its defence detachments from his company & convalescents from the 4th Regt. The Block house on the point is entrusted to [Lieutenant Fowler] and will be garrisoned by detachments of Artillery—Light Troops under Lt. Coll Appling and Capt Sproulls will take post in the ravine near the Asst Inspr Genl's Marque and will receive orders from the General. The Light Artillery will take such position as will best anoy the Column of the Enemy, keeping up constantly a brisk fire on them[;] they will also take post when not employed, in the same ravine with the light troops.

Mr. Paris, Captain of the Artificers will form a corps of Rocketeers with his men[.] They will take the directions of the Chief Engineer. The artillery is to be considered a Separate Service and the officers of that arme [sic] are responsible only to the Comd Genl for the correct exercise of their functions. The officers of engineers will give directions for additional defences and for repairs, as occasion may require, which will be the duty of the several Commandants to give all the aid in their power to execute. thus every man knowing his post & his duty, can have no excuse to execute it with firmness and decision.

General Mooers stationed 250 militia near Culver's Hill, just south of where the British right column was expected. Macomb cautioned Mooers regarding the untested militiamen. They were to fire their weapons before retiring; they had to experience the action of battle, the sounds and smells of war. With the lake road being wet and soft, the British left column was not expected to advance as quickly as the column approaching Beekmantown. In the early afternoon, Aikin's volunteers were sent through the woods to the Dead Creek. Once there, the boys were asked to place themselves under the command of Colonel Appling. Wanting to retain their autonomy, the boys voted among themselves to return to the village and seek additional weapons from the cantonment. Not all the boys were armed; some had family weapons—muskets and bird rifles. At the cantonment, they would be given military weapons and ammunition as had been ordered by General Macomb. In the evening, Major Wool and 250 regulars joined the force at Culver's Hill. Williams was now called on to provide reports of the enemy day and night. At ten o'clock in the morning of the same day, with the latest news of the enemy movements, Macdonough alerted the fleet to prepare for orders. A half hour later, he issued the order for the ships to warp (move without sail by oar or dragging anchor) into line. Macomb ordered rockets sent to Cumberland Head and Dead Creek with an instructional letter to General Mooers that they be used as an advance signal should the enemy be sighted. The letter described the proper procedures in employing a rocket and was accompanied by a labeled sketch itemizing a rocket's features and terms. While the British had some experience with rockets before Plattsburgh, to the Americans of the northern army and the local militia, the weapon was a new, high-tech introduction—hence the instructions to Mooers.[8]

The American forces thus deployed, they would wait for the morning and the sound of the British musicians announcing assembly and the march. Musicians, including many young boys, were the mass-communication means on land and aboard ship. The shrill tones of fife or bugle or the crisp snaps of a side drum carried orders in the confusion and smoke of battle. At Plattsburgh, fife and drum were the primary instruments of the American forces; the British army came with buglers also. The boy musicians of the American forces at Plattsburgh served with the consent of their parents or guardians. General Macomb, earlier in the spring, had ordered that "boys and men learning music" practice for seven hours a day. One thirteen-year-old American drummer deserted from his duties with the Fourteenth Infantry. The order for his apprehension states that Charles W. Rogers was a drummer "who beats remarkably well on the drum for a boy of his age."[9]

On September 6, at daybreak and as expected, the British advance broke into two columns. General Power's brigade, half of General Robinson's brigade, part of General Brisbane's brigade and four light companies took the road to the right toward Beekmantown. The remainder of the force under Robinson's command, including the remainder of General Brisbane's brigade, was to proceed through the Cedar Swamps near the lake. Robinson wrote, "The worst I had ever seen—bad by nature, and rendered extremely dangerous by the breaking of old logs, with which a kind of causeway had been formed many years before. Scarcely a horse got through without losing a shoe, and the artillery stuck fast for three hours." With them they brought an initial complement of artillery: "three Light 6 Pounder Brigades complete,

"Culver Hill: September 6, 1814." John J. Purdy, 2007. *War of 1812 Museum, Battle of Plattsburgh Association. Used with permission.*

Two Light Bass [*sic*: brass] 24 pdr Guns, one 8 inch Brass Howitzer and three 24 pdr Carronades, all mounted on Travelling Carriages." One Light Six-Pounder Brigade was left at Chazy.[10]

Throughout the night and into the early morning of the sixth, as the military provisions were moved from Levi Platt's barn to the forts, American militia continued to join the force at Culver's Hill. At daybreak, they numbered seven hundred. At seven o'clock in the morning, after marching through Beekmantown, Power's column approached the waiting militia and regulars. There was a brief exchange of gunfire in which Colonel Wellington of the Third Buffs, a nephew of Lord Wellington, was killed. As the action began to heat up, a company of New York dragoons appeared on the north hillside. With their red coats, the militia mistook them for British, exciting a panic and causing the militia to believe that the British were flanking them. A rout began toward Plattsburgh even as the officers and many of their own ranks urged the retreating men to stand their ground. Power's column pressed onward toward Plattsburgh. Wool's thinning force fell back in front of the British column, finding cover behind the fences and trees of the roadway. John C. Rochester described the actions that day: "We had opportunity of lying behind stone fences & secreting in the wood—until they would arrive within gun shot—when we would open fire & retire about a half mile at the time—in this manner we fought them for six miles when their main force arrived & we were compelled to give up one half the town—on the north side of Saranac river." Aikin's rifle company, now fully armed, passed through the retreating militia on the roadway entering the village and took a position near Mr. Halsey's house.

Bathurst wrote to General Ross on this day, directing that after the Chesapeake actions were completed, he was to withdraw his troops and move south, annoying the towns along the American coast, gathering more troops from the islands and entering the Gulf Coast to conduct the final diversionary act of the plan: an attack on New Orleans.[11]

General Macomb had ordered Captain Leonard to take a detachment and three cannons to Halsey's Corners, near the Platt farm on the Beekmantown road. As the retreating militia streamed forward, the regulars accompanying the artillery masked the three weapons that had been placed in the middle of the roadway. As the British column came within range of the cannons, the American regulars made their way to the stone wall at

"Close Quarters at Halsey's Corners." John J. Purdy, 2011. *War of 1812 Museum, Battle of Plattsburgh Association. Used with permission.*

"An American Regular." John J. Purdy, 2008. *Author's private collection.*

"Old Stone Mill." *From the* Pictorial Field Book of the War of 1812.

the roadside, where Aikin's volunteers and others were sheltered.

The artillery fired three times as those behind the walls added their rifle fire. In the words of Jeremiah Barnes, second sergeant of Captain Sherry's company, "Once with balls—and twice with grape and canister, mowing the British down in great numbers, who however immediately closed up their lines each time, and after the third discharge made a dash and captured one of the guns." Amos Barber, present at the scene, said many years later that the second firing by Leonard "cut off the right legs of sixteen men." Barnes's recollection of the casualties from the two engagements was as follows: "Wellington [*sic*: Willington] and a lieut. [Ensign Chapman] of the 3d Buffs and 2 lieuts. of the 58th killed, and one capt. & one lieut. of the 58th light company wounded, together with about 100 privates killed and wounded; while that on our part did not exceed twenty five." The American force followed the militia in its retreat across the Saranac River. Once on the south side of the river and in a more favorable geographical advantage, it believed it would be able to hold the British advance.

Aikin's boys moved to join Wool's men in opposing the invaders, but the British column advanced so quickly that it occupied the roadway into the village. Isolated from Wool's force and prevented from using the roadway, the boys went west and south, crossing the river at a point above the newer bridge at Winchel's Mill. Once across the river, Aikin's company proceeded into the village and positioned itself in the old mill, near the village bridge; they remained in the village for the day, joining the action and firing at the British on the opposite bank of the river. Heavy firing was present throughout the day. As the

At the mill, September 6, 1814. *From Panel 1, City of Plattsburgh Heritage Trail. Lee Hunt, 1993. Used with permission.*

action slowed, Sherry's company withdrew to the Salmon River settlement, where General Mooers maintained his headquarters.[12]

When news of Power's approaching column was transmitted to Appling and Sproul at the Dead Creek, they immediately withdrew along the shore road and crossed the Saranac, joining in the defense of the village. By eleven o'clock in the morning, the British were firmly in control of the village north of the Saranac, and the remainder of the right column proceeded into the village. The British force began its encampment on the broad hillcrest stretching east to west about a mile north of the village center. Macomb assigned the Vermont militia to posts west along the river and sent Captain Vaughan with two companies to Wait's Mill at the west road.

The *Eagle* log notes that the British burned several houses, but there is no British account of such action taking place. From the deck of the *Eagle*, it must have appeared so, but American accounts indicate that homes on the northern side of the river were intentionally targeted with hotshot to remove cover for British sharpshooters.[13]

The action slows, September 6, 1814. *From Panel 1, City of Plattsburgh Heritage Trail. Lee Hunt, 1993. Used with permission.*

The left column, after being delayed by the obstacles and soft terrain on the lake road, reached the northern end of Cumberland Bay in the late afternoon. Robinson and Brisbane, with the artillery and baggage, entered onto the roadway parallel to the Dead Creek. The area had been abandoned by the American forces after they partially dismantled the bridge across the creek. Macdonough's gunboats fired on them for a short while until the column's artillery and rockets were brought up to repel the gunboats. The British guns and rockets took their toll on the crew of the American vessels. Lieutenant Silas Duncan fell, his arm torn by a British rocket, and several men died from artillery fire. Once the American vessels retired, the Royal Sappers and Miners repaired the bridge, and the column moved toward the village. "His Gunboats alone left to defend the Ford and to prevent our restoring the Bridges which had been imperfectly destroyed, an inconvenience soon surmounted," Prevost would tell Bathurst. Entering the village, they found that the Americans had crossed to the south side of the Saranac River by both village bridges and had removed the bridge planking, a result of General Macomb's order.[14]

As Robinson entered the limits of the village, the British quartermaster general asked if the troops would be able to attack immediately if they removed and left their packs, thus enabling the men to maneuver more easily. Robinson asked if the American territory had been reconnoitered, and upon receiving word that it had not, he advised General Prevost that any plan for attack should be delayed until particulars of the American fortresses and river fords were known. He indicated that, tactically, any attempt to cross the river should be made at daybreak, with the troops at

Prelude to Battle (September 1–10, 1814)

Make ready, September 6, 1814. *From Panel 1, City of Plattsburgh Heritage Trail. Lee Hunt, 1993. Used with permission.*

"Repulse at the Stone Mill." *From* Our Country: A Household History of the United States, *vol. 2.*

the ready before the sun came up. The American forces continued their defense throughout the afternoon with artillery fire from the fortifications and musket fire from the south bank of the Saranac. Prevost made his way to the farm of Edward V. Allen on the highest point overlooking the village and declared Allen's home his headquarters. The home was located

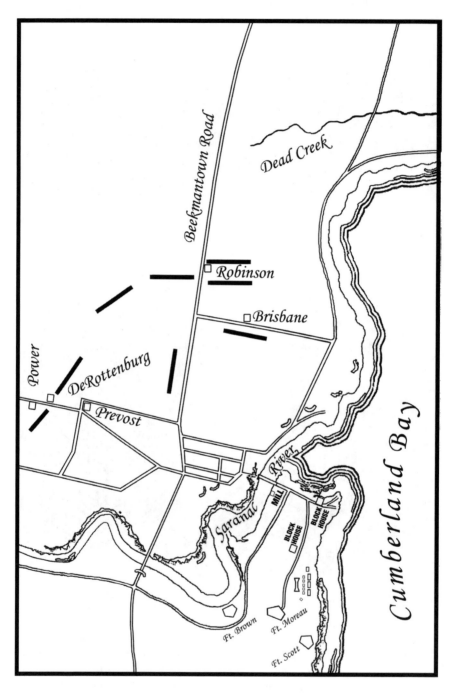

American and British forces in the village of Plattsburgh. *Adapted by Elyse Zielinski, 2012.*

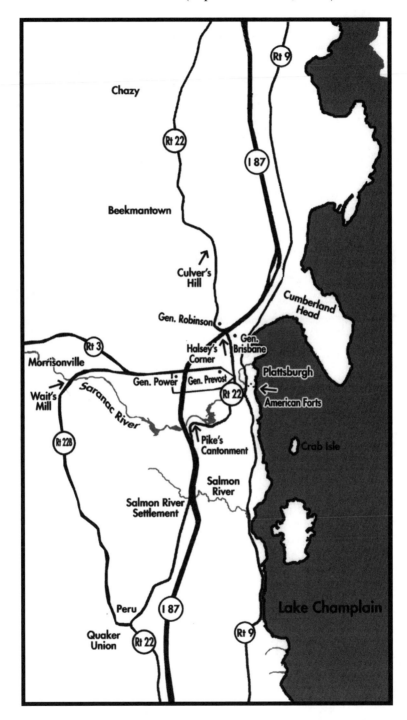

The battlefield today. *Adapted by Elyse Zielinski.*

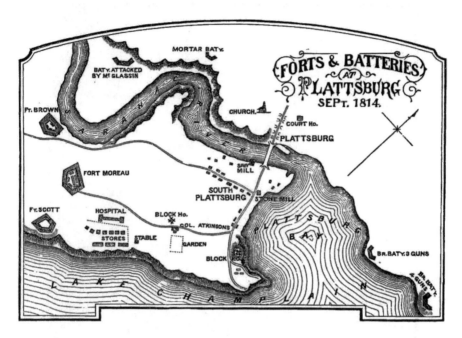

"Forts & Batteries at Plattsburg Sept. 1814." *From the* Pictorial Field Book of the War of 1812.

near the present intersection of Cornelia and Broad Streets and offered a
commanding view of the American fortifications. There before him was the
challenge: "They consisted of three redoubts, two small blockhouses, and a
battery of heavy guns towards the lake. The redoubts were not finished, and
the guns of the principal one were all en barbette, and consequently might
be easily silenced during an assault." Lieutenant Lang of the Nineteenth
Light Dragoons reported that the American works were not built "within
established rules"; they were sand berms faced with wood board, the interior
being open without shelters and the bastions arranged to sweep the trenches
surrounding them. It was observed that the American fleet at anchor in the
bay was within gun range of the American defenses on the south side of the
Saranac River. Macdonough's vessels were moored at anchor within range
of long guns if the British were to place a battery at Sailly's Point.[15]

In occupying Plattsburgh, Major General De Rottenburg, the commander
of the British Left Division, established his headquarters just to the east of
Power at the current site of the intersection of Interstate Route 87 and
Route 3. Power, responsible for the west flank, established his headquarters
near the Hammond Farm to the west of De Rottenburg and some three

miles outside the village. Robinson positioned his troops just north of the village and above Brisbane's location. The British encampment stretched from the northwestern side of Cumberland Bay westward for nearly four miles. Prevost, satisfied with his position and strength deployment, directed the placement of batteries. The Royal Sappers and Miners were set to the task of building the structures. The British commander ordered the rest of the artillery to be advanced to Plattsburgh. Seeing the strength of the fortifications and batteries on the south side of the river, he called for an additional two eight-inch mortars and two iron twelve-pounders. These guns would complete the artillery complement for his own batteries. Robinson's troops were gathering ladders, which could be used to scale the American works. Macomb, in later describing the day to General Jonathan Williams, stated that the British "quietly encamped before the village."

Eleazer Williams wrote of the predicament in which the American army was now placed:

There was no prospect of retaining their position against such overwhelming force as that of the enemy. They had been compelled to recede about six miles before such a cloud of skirmishers and a heavy column of the enemy, as to impress

British occupy the DeLord House, September 6, 1814. *From Panel 2, City of Plattsburgh Heritage Trail. Lee Hunt, 1993. Used with permission.*

them with an idea of their own weakness, and their inability to withstand the invaders. This was not only extremely disheartening, but humiliating to the American soldiery. General Macomb was silent and thoughtful—he saw too much, no doubt, of his dangerous position—but the garrisons were committed to him for safe keeping, and he would defend them to the last extremity, or be buried under them. General Mooers' division are bivouacked at Salmon river. His advance-guard extends to Pike's encampment on the Saranac.

In closing his journal entry, Williams was quite complimentary toward Aikin's volunteers, saying, "There is no corps more useful and watchful than the one under the command of Captain Aikens and Lieutenant Flagg."[16]

In the late evening and under cover of darkness, Macdonough ordered the fleet to warp to the southward about a half mile from its anchored position, with Crab Island then being approximately one and a half miles to the south-southeast. On the seventh, the surprised British general staff awoke to find that Macdonough's fleet had moved. Anchored farther south and east than the day before, Macdonough was outside the range of the new British battery near Sailly's Point. The new anchor closed any approach to the bay from the south (an entrance from the south would come between the guns of Fort Scott and Macdonough's fleet). The fleet's new position forced an entrance into the bay between the rocks of Crab Island and those of the southern tip of Cumberland Head.

Aikin's volunteers aided the forces at the blockhouse near Gravelly Point (the present-day eastern ends of Dock and Bridge Streets) before

returning to the Salmon River Settlement in the evening. The blockhouse was across the mouth of the Saranac River from the DeLord Store and the new British battery established near the DeLord house.

There were skirmishes along the river throughout the day, the worst of which left American Lieutenant Runk of the Sixth Infantry injured by musket fire; he died

British artillery at the DeLord House, September 6, 1814. *From Panel 2, City of Plattsburgh Heritage Trail. Lee Hunt, 1993. Used with permission.*

the following day. Runk would be the only American land officer to die in the fighting at Plattsburgh.[17]

On this day, when Captain Downie of the *Confiance* wrote to General Prevost that he was still two days from being ready to sail to Chazy, Macdonough, still shy of full crews, requested more soldiers from Macomb. The army general balked at any further assignments from his meager forces; he had a group

Field gun. *Author's sketch.*

of boys helping to defend the blockhouse on the point! He did agree to allow Lieutenant Joseph Smith to select from among the prisoners in the pioneer crews. Macdonough thus gained almost forty men who were assigned to the *Eagle* and drilled as members of its gun crews.

Prevost, upon receiving Downie's communication, informed Robinson that "the troops should remain in their present position until further orders"; they would wait for the British naval force before attacking. The British batteries were initially armed with the twenty-four-pound carronades, light twenty-four-pound brass guns, twelve-pound iron ship guns and the eight-inch howitzer. The largest British invasion force to exist on the American continent during the war was preparing to move as the secretary of war, General John Armstrong, resigned his office.[18]

General Mooers assigned Captain Sherry's militia company from the Salmon River settlement to stand with Captain Vaughan's company at Wait's Mill and the "upper bridge" on the West Road (the present-day location of Route 22B and its crossing of the Saranac at Morrisonville). They would report on the western movements of the British for the next several days. Power sent his picket under the command of Captain Noadie west to establish a boundary. They encountered Vaughan's force of twenty-three at the bridge near Wait's Mill. After a brief encounter, the British picket withdrew with the loss of "two killed and several wounded." Three volunteers from Sherry's company would afterward cross to the northern side of the river and move north through the woods. They discovered that the British had also established an outlying picket at Cadyville and were patrolling the Plank Road leading to the village of Plattsburgh.

The encounter with the British western picket force so far outside the village brought Macomb to realize that Prevost might attempt to flank and attack from the south. The British had been to the site of Pike's former cantonment area when they destroyed its barracks in the late spring raid of 1813. The cantonment area's location, unused by the American forces for over a year and a half, suddenly became, again, strategically important in the defense of Plattsburgh. Macomb ordered that the roadways leading from the cantonment to the village be disguised and obstructed. The work was to be accomplished at night, without firelight, so as not to alert the enemy to the activity. Macomb was, as Pierre Berton describes him, intelligent, imaginative, long on acumen and a believer of military deception.[19]

Eleazer Williams noted the first arrivals of the Vermont militia on the eighth: "Captain Farnsworth, of St. Albans, with his rifle company, ninety-six strong." Aikin's volunteer rifle company moved from the Salmon River settlement to the forts. The wind became increasingly gustier, and rain fell throughout the day, causing Macdonough's fleet to mind its anchors. In the lull afforded by the weather, General Mooers issued the following statements in an order from his headquarters:

> *The General is determined to have all deserters punished in the most exemplary manner, and all officers and others are directed to bring back such as are attempting to escape. Those brave men of the militia and volunteer corps, who manfully kept their posts and fought the enemy on their retreat before a far superior force, for the distance of nearly seven miles, deserve the General's warmest thanks, and the love and gratitude of their country. The cool, intrepid and admirable skill and good order displayed by the small detachment of less than three hundred regulars, under the excellent officer Major Wool was highly honorable to themselves, and furnishes an example worthy of our future imitation.*
>
> *The General cannot avoid noticing that the determined resistance by Capt. Vaughan and his small band, at the upper Bridge, which obliged a much superior force of the enemy to retire with loss, was both honorable to himself and the men under his command. Captain Aikin's Company of Riflemen, and others of the volunteers have displayed throughout, a degree of gallantry in opposing the enemy, and of enterprise and boldness in reconnoitering him under all circumstances...*
>
> *Let every man strive to do his duty at this crisis, as it will be much easier to retain our present position than to regain it after it is lost.*

The overpowering strength of the British numbers brought Macomb to the realization that he must practice as much as puffery, smoke and mirrors, as possible. He had to psychologically increase the size of his force in the eyes of the enemy. Hereafter, Macomb would parade the troops in full view of the British at each change of guard. In the evenings, to draw attention away from the ongoing work at the western cantonment roadways and to create a clear view of his advance ground before the British, Macomb would order buildings burned. With troops parading at night, the young general sought to complete the illusion that reinforcements were arriving day and night. To reinforce the visual perception, he allowed it to be known that ten thousand militiamen were expected to fill the woods south of the Saranac.[20]

Near deaf from the guns. *From Panel 1, City of Plattsburgh Heritage Trail. Lee Hunt, 1993. Used with permission.*

September 8 was a day of less-adversarial tasks for the British, as well. Brevet Lieutenant Colonel H. Roberts of the Buffs petitioned General Prevost for the promotion of junior officers to fill the vacancies left by the deaths of Lieutenant Colonel Willington and Ensign Chapman. Prevost communicated to Downie the existing anchored position of the American vessels within Cumberland Bay and his plan for the coming battle. Prevost indicated that the ground forces were waiting for Downie's vessels before an attack would be made. Downie replied, as he had previously, that the *Confiance* was not ready to see battle; he would anchor at Chazy until his guns were made ready. Downie was now confident that the *Confiance* alone would be the match for the American fleet.[21]

With the coming of a clear day, actions on both sides increased. Williams spoke of being near deaf from the firing of the American guns on the British positions. Throughout the day, there was a constant cracking heard as sharpshooters discharged their weapons at targets on opposite sides of the river. The sounds of war continued from daylight to dusk. "Day and night we skirmished at several bridges and fords to prevent his light troops getting in our rear," Macomb would later write. On the day on which volunteers from Vermont began to stream into New York, eight hundred from Charlotte in the afternoon alone, another detachment of British tested the forces at Wait's Mill but were repelled as before.

The boys of Aikin's company took time on this clear September 9 to bury one of their own, Peters, who had been killed in the previous day's fighting. Eleazer Williams, impressed by the actions of these young volunteers, said of them, "[They] are not only useful in watching our front line, but they are brave and daring in skirmishing with the enemy." He spoke of the youthful, or perhaps foolish, bravado in three of their number (Allen, Travers and Williams) crossing the river to spy on the British and stopping to unearth spirits known to them to be hidden in a nearby barn. They were discovered by the British and fired upon, escaping back across the river under the cover of their comrades' fire.[22]

From inside Fort Moreau, John C. Rochester wrote to his father, "We are now in our forts almost surrounded by a very large force of the enemy—our force is not far from 3,000 effectives—the enemies sd. To be about 7,000." In fact, the numbers were greater than they thought; the British force had grown to over 10,000. General De Rottenburg's report of the previous day shows the British troop strength at 10,351, and with them they had 648 horses. In Macomb's words, "The militia had collected under General Moores to the amount of about 700—our regular force did not exceed 1500 for duty—five hundred were constantly fighting and the rest working to complete the defenses of our position." Rochester's apprehension was evidenced in his thoughts that, without reinforcements, and with the British coming from all quarters, "we shall have a bloody battle."

William Gilliland reported to General Mooers that he had arms for 150 of Mooers's volunteers at his home near the mouth of the Salmon River. Approximately 550 Vermont militia had massed near Gilliland's home before the afternoon was over, and he passed on to Mooers the expectation of 600 more arriving before morning.

The longer the enemy delayed, the better the fortifications could be constructed. The American forces continued enhancing the defensive strengths of their fortifications. Inside the unfinished Fort Moreau, the small force had not paused in their tasks to address their own comforts; all was focused on their defense. Rochester wrote, "Without even a tent—the officers all compelled to lie on the parapet of the fort."[23]

The wait annoyed Prevost; he knew the advantages gained by the Americans. "I need not dwell with you on the evils resulting to both services from delay," he wrote to Downie at Chazy. In the same communication, Downie learned of Macdonough's manning shortage for the new brig (*Eagle*) and that it had been partially addressed by drawing men from the American prisoner ranks. Prevost was so concerned of learning immediately of Downie's availability that he issued an order to Captain Watson of the Provincial Cavalry "to remain at the Chazy until you are preparing to get underweigh [*sic*]…instantly to return to this place with the intelligence."

American officers aboard the *Saratoga. From Panel 4, City of Plattsburgh Heritage Trail. Lee Hunt, 1993. Used with permission.*

Captain Watson didn't have to remain at Chazy for any length of time, as on the same day Downie penned the following to Prevost:

> *I have the Honour to communicate to Your Excel'cy that it is my intention to weigh and proceed from this anchorage about midnight, in the expectation of rounding into the Bay of Plattsburg about dawn of day, & commence an immediate attack upon the Enemy, if they should be found anchored in a position that offer a chance of success. I rely on any assistance you can afford the Squadron. In manning the Flotilla & ships, finding we are many short, I have made application the Officer Commanding at Chazy for a Company of the 39th Regt. I have the honour of Your Excelly's letter of this morning to which the proceeding is a full answer.*[24]

That evening, just before midnight, volunteer members from the American Fifteenth Regiment and William's Rangers led by Captain M'Glassin executed a raid across the Saranac. They destroyed what Eleazer Williams described as a British bomb battery under construction near Waite's Printing Office and within range of Fort Brown, M'Glassin succeeding in spiking the guns. Everest describes the site as a British blockhouse under construction. Fitz-Enz states that the battery contained "six and ten-pound rockets." Macomb's map indicates the presence of the gun battery, but no blockhouse, at the location. The map also shows the British rocket battery to be several hundred yards to the northwest of this gun battery, on the south side of present-day Broad Street.

The weather would not cooperate in Downie's plan. Late evening breezes being absent, the prospect of an entire sail fleet "in irons" having to be towed or warped southward against the northern-flowing Lake Champlain currents did not sit well with Downie. The delay compounded the frustration existing in the relationship between Downie and Prevost. Receiving the news that Downie would not appear at Cumberland Head as he had been advised, Prevost wrote again to Downie, essentially complaining that the troops had been ready since 6:00 a.m. to "storm the Enemy's works at nearly the same moment as the Naval Action should commence in the Bay."

As the weather improved throughout the day, the order was again given. The British troops would be ready to move at sunrise on the following morning.[25]

General Samuel Strong from Vermont arrived on the tenth to join the expanding number of militia from that state encamped on the sand plain adjacent to the Saranac River's hillside that had once been Pike's cantonment. The morning report of the Thirty-sixth Regiment of the New York Militia at the Salmon River settlement under the command of Colonel Thomas Miller shows 243 fit for duty and 60 missing; no report had been received that morning for Aikin's volunteers.

Macdonough's fleet continued to make preparations for battle...and waited. Macomb's forces continued to strengthen the fortifications and hide roadways leading from Pike's cantonment toward the village...and waited. Prevost...waited.[26]

7
The Battles at Plattsburgh (September 11, 1814)

With a north wind about him, Downie proceeded from his anchor at Chazy in the early morning hours of September 11. The approach of the *Confiance* and its flotilla was detected by Macdonough's guard boat at seven o'clock and relayed to the waiting American fleet. Aboard Macdonough's vessels, the musicians signaled the crews to quarters, and final preparations were made for battle.

Shortly before eight o'clock in the morning, Downie's fleet approached the northern end of Cumberland Head. According to the arranged plan, he ordered the guns scaled, signaling his approach and what was to be the commencement of Prevost's ground assault. Robinson was called to the British headquarters, where the attack plan was communicated to the ground commanders. General Brisbane's brigade would busy the Americans at the two bridge locations within the village and across the Saranac between them, "creating a diversion in favor of the column under Major General Robinson." The batteries would open fire as the British ships engaged the American fleet, and the Quartermaster's Department would lead the bulk of the ground troops and their artillery across the river at the ford adjacent to what was Pike's old cantonment. They would attempt to gain the American left flank and the rear of Macomb's unfinished fortifications.

An hour passed while Prevost met with his field commanders. The lack of communication within the British camp became evident immediately. Prevost was told that, for lack of transportation, the heavy twelve-pounders had not arrived. Perhaps more disappointing for him was the fact that even if the cannons had arrived, they would be useless, as no battery had been prepared for them. Downie's fleet was just rounding Cumberland Head as the meeting concluded. Although Prevost would later tell Bathurst that he immediately ordered the troops to advance upon seeing Downie's fleet enter the bay, General Robinson quotes Prevost as directing, "It is now nine o'clock, march off at ten." The movement of the British ground troops would not occur for another hour.

It must have been in the casual atmosphere of the September Sunday morning that Prevost wrote to Bathurst:

> *Upon the arrival of the Reinforcements from the Garroane I lost no time in assembling three Brigades on the Frontier of Lower Canada extending from the River Richelleu to the St. Lawrence and in forming them into a Division under the command of Major General de Rottenburg for the purpose of carrying into effect His Royal Highness, the Prince Regent's commands which had been conveyed to me by Your Lordship in Your Dispatch of 3ᵈ of June last.*

Robinson waited and watched the two opposing naval fleets from his ridge-top location. At 9:30 a.m., as the action in the bay commenced, Robinson directed his demi brigade, the First Battalion, Seventy-sixth, and Third Battalion, Twenty-seventh, to march west by the northern side of the ridge above the village, in so doing hiding the movement from the American view. As his column marched westward, Robinson observed, "Before I left the spot I could perceive showers of grape-shot falling about the 'Confiance' in every direction." His long-distance observation of the *Confiance* led him to believe that, aboard the great ship, "two thirds of her guns on the larboard side were either dismounted or disabled."

Two columns began their advance within the village toward the American forces on the south side of the Saranac River. Eleazer Williams described the initial onslaught, "When they arrived at the brink of the river, they were saluted with such a storm of shot and grape from our battery, as to compel them to fall back, and make their way into the houses, shops, barns, and ditches."

At ten o'clock, Robinson's column would meet with the Third Brigade at Power's location several miles west of the village bordering the Hammond Farm (today, on Route 3 west of Plattsburgh and beyond Interstate Route 87). The farm's location was instrumental in leading to the recent archaeological find of Pike's cantonment lying almost due south of it. Likewise, the significance of the positive location of the cantonment is key in understanding the land movements of the British and the expanse of the

The Battles at Plattsburgh (September 11, 1814)

"Battle of Plattsburgh." *After Alonzo Chapelle, Johnson, Fry & Co., 1858.*

battlefield. Due south of the cantonment was the location of what was the settlement at Salmon River, Mooers's headquarters.[1]

The action on the bay was to be a spectator event for the locals who stayed in the area. As many as three hundred gathered on the western shore of Cumberland Head, according to Daniel Dusten, then sixteen. The scene that would play out in front of them promised to be a lifetime memory. Approximately 181 cannons would float before them in the largest naval engagement Lake Champlain would ever experience. Although the British had control of the roads into the village, including the Lake Road along the Dead Creek, the locals went northeast and entered onto Cumberland Head by the Woodruff Pond, avoiding the British picket guard.[2]

Macdonough's fleet was just off the northwest point of Crab Island, at anchor and in a line slightly northeast to southwest; *Eagle* was to the north, then *Saratoga, Ticonderoga* and *Preble* to the south, all out of range of the British guns. In that position, Macdonough knew that if Downie did come into the bay, he had only two means of entry: by going south around Crab Island, bearing north between the island and the mainland shore, leaving him little maneuvering room between the shore and the island and dangerously close to the guns of Fort Scott or going straight into the bay, avoiding the rocky underwater topography of Cumberland Head and Crab Island, directly

Above: "Battles of Lake Champlain, and Plattsburgh." *From* History of the Late War Between the United States and Great Britain.

Left: *"Commodore Thomas MacDonough."* Violet Bernstein, 1977. *War of 1812 Museum, Battle of Plattsburgh Association. Used with permission.*

into range of Macdonough's waiting carronade broadsides. In choosing the latter, Downie would play into Macdonough's plan. The deck guns of both fleets would soon spew forth their iron loads in a thunderous two hours of smoke-filled horror.

Macdonough waited as the British bore up into what they thought would be a north wind inside the bay. The steady north breeze that had filled Downie's sails on the open lake now caused the twenty-three-foot white ensign of the *Confiance* to baffle in the confounding mix of eddies inside the bay. The north–south current within the bay runs counter to the lake's south–north current. The combination of the unexpected wind pattern and the contra-current frustrated Downie's ability to maneuver to anchor. As soon as the British fleet was within range of the *Saratoga's* guns, Macdonough opened fire, his first broadside raking the *Confiance's* deck.

Even in the hail of Macdonough's guns, Downie pressed his fleet on without firing until he was able to anchor opposite Macdonough's. Their line from the north was *Chubb, Linnet, Confiance* and then *Finch*. The British fleet, with its complement of thirty long twenty-four-pounders could have stood off in the deeper waters of the broad lake outside the bay and beyond the effective range of all but Macdonough's fourteen long twenty-fours.

"McDonough Pointing the Gun." *From* Battles of America by Sea and Land.

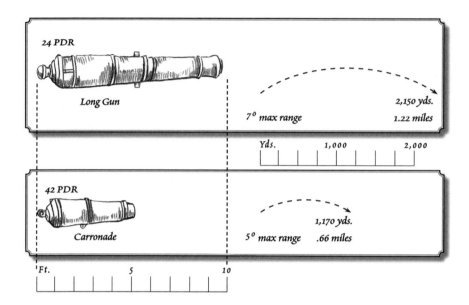

24 PDR

Long Gun

7° max range

2,150 yds.
1.22 miles

Yds.   1,000   2,000

42 PDR

Carronade

5° max range   .66 miles

1,170 yds.

Ft.   5   10

Above: Cannon and carronade. *Adapted by Elyse Zielinski, 2012.*

Left: "The Battle of Lake Champlain." *From* Sea Power in Its Relations to the War of 1812.

Downie's agreement with Prevost and his own bravado led him to engage at close range within the bay.

Almost immediately, the effect of his decision for close action was apparent. The British fleet was completely within range of Macdonough's twenty-nine thirty-two-pound carronades (British: thirteen) and six forty-two-pound carronades (British: zero). Downie's sheet anchor, made ready by the stopper, was shot off its cathead in the first American broadsides from the *Saratoga*. "When the spare Anchor was let go, the Cable was shot away—the best bower was then let go, the spring on which suffered the same fate," Lieutenant Joseph Robertson would recall. Downie, his ship finally anchored, directed the first broadsides from the *Confiance* but was killed within fifteen minutes.

Command aboard the British flagship became the responsibility of Lieutenant Robertson, who took the helm of a vessel that was "sixteen days before, on the Stocks, with an unorganized Crew, comprised of several Drafts of Men; who had recently arrived from different ships at Quebec, many of whom only joined the day before, and were totally unknown either to the Officers or to each other, with the want of Gun Locks as well as other necessary appointments, not to be procured in this Country."

Robertson attempted to inform Captain Pring aboard the *Linnet* (the officer to whom fleet command would have devolved) of the death of Captain Downie. Finding that the ship's signal book could not be located and the *Confiance*'s two gigs had been shot from the stern, Robertson could not communicate with Pring. Robertson assumed command of the *Confiance* and took control of the deck, directing the ship's gunfire. While the *Confiance* did have rockets aboard, there is no evidence that Robertson made use of them in the battle.

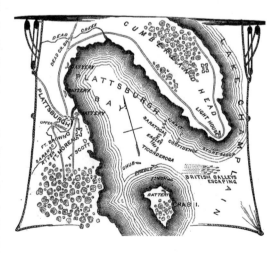

The ten-gun *Chubb* (formerly the American *Growler*) was severely damaged almost immediately: cables destroyed and bowsprit, main boom and most of its standing rigging shot away. Unable to maneuver and

"Plan of the Naval Action on Lake Champlain." *From the* Pictorial Field Book of the War of 1812.

pushed by the current, it drifted down the line of fire southward (eventually being taken in tow by American gunboats at 10:00 a.m.).[3]

Macdonough observed:

> *He anchored in a line ahead, at about 300 yards distance from my line; his ship opposed to the* Saratoga, *his brig to the* Eagle, *Captain Robert Henley, his galleys, thirteen in number, to the schooner, sloop, and a division of our galleys; one of his sloops assisting their ship and brig, the other assisting their galleys. Our remaining galleys with the* Saratoga *and* Eagle. *In this situation, the whole force, on both sides, became engaged; the* Saratoga *suffering much from the heavy fire of the* Confiance. *I could perceive at the same time, however, that our fire was very destructive to her.*[4]

The *Saratoga*'s crew worked well under Lieutenant Peter Gamble's direction, carrying out their tasks as they had been trained to do in the preceding weeks. Macdonough worked with his crew in the frenzy of battle. "He had frequently to work his own guns, when his men at them were shot; and three times he was driven across the deck by splinters."

The *Saratoga* deck at close action. *From Panel 4, City of Plattsburgh Heritage Trail. Lee Hunt, 1993. Used with permission.*

The Battles at Plattsburgh (September 11, 1814)

Macdonough commands the deck of the *Saratoga*. *Johnson, Fry & Co., 1866.*

Judge Julius C. Hubbel of Chazy is said to have met with Macdonough on the *Saratoga*'s debris-strewn deck shortly after the battle concluded. He tells of Macdonough relating the details of a boom cut in two, its falling parts knocking the American commandant to the deck. Macdonough would remember the cool transfer of charge when Lieutenant Gamble was struck and died. He praised Sail Master Brum and Purser Mr. Beale for the manner in which they carried orders across the deck and assisted with the guns. Certain paintings of the period depict for us the conditions of the naval battle at its height. Perhaps the best representation of the naval action at Plattsburgh is the stunning J.O. Davidson rendering, *The Battle of Lake Champlain*, which hangs in the Key Bank Gallery of the Battle of Plattsburgh Association's War of 1812 Museum.

Then a lieutenant, Joseph Smith would years later recount the horrors of the day. The *Eagle*'s deck had been raked by British cannon, and the spring lines had been shot away, complicating the ability to wind (turn) ship. Smith was knocked off a gun struck by a British ball. Falling to the deck, he struck his head and was unconscious for a period of time. He said that he had assigned the wife of one of the musicians to a position near the magazine, as safe a position as he could find for her, and later, he witnessed her carrying cartridges across the deck to the gun crews, her husband having been killed. However, according to the muster rolls, the four musicians assigned to Macdonough's vessels survived. The recollections of Smith were related in 1875, shortly before

"The Battle of Lake Champlain." Julian Davidson, 1894. *War of 1812 Museum, Battle of Plattsburgh Association. Used with permission.*

his death. He is said to have forgotten the name of the woman and the soldier killed. Perhaps Smith's recollections were clouded by time. No data has been found to corroborate the presence of women on any of Macdonough's vessels.

The *Saratoga* was set on fire by hotshot from the enemy's ship, we're told. The British would later deny the firing of hotshot from the *Confiance*, but the existence of a furnace aboard their vessel was reported previously by Caleb Nichols and confirmed upon capture.[5]

At 10:00 a.m., the eleven-gun sloop *Finch* (formerly the American *Eagle*), with its rudder inoperative and sails torn by the exchange of fire with the *Preble*, began to drift south uncontrollably. As the crew of the *Finch* labored to bring its guns again to bear against the *Preble*, it was exposed to a raking fire that injured many of its crew and caused confusion on the deck. The *Preble* was being pursued by the British gunboats but soon mercifully drifted into the shadow of the *Saratoga*. The *Preble*'s boatswain had been killed, and its sailing master had been severely wounded. It began to move off northwest toward shore and out of the action. Charles Budd reported of the damage:

> *The* Preble *I have the pleasure to state is not materially impaired— She has got 2 eighteen pound shot through her hull about a foot from the wa*[les]*—her larboard wales considerably marked—1 eighteen pound shot lodged in her stern, having carried away the head knees and* [slit] *the stem—one 24 pd shot through her quarter bulwarks & the dents of two 18pd shot from the* Finch's Columbiads.

The British gunboats retired to assist the *Finch*. Twice, the commander of the *Finch*, Lieutenant Hicks, attempted to bear northwest to engage the

Ticonderoga. Taking on water from three-shot that pierced its hull below the water line and unable to effect a return into the action, Hicks attempted to move out into the lake. With the main boom badly damaged and sails and rigging cut, he wound up on a path onto the rocks at the north point of Crab Island and within range of the American six-pound guns placed there. Despite the efforts of the British crew to lighten the load to float free their vessel, the *Finch* was hopelessly grounded. In the court-martial that would follow, Hicks and the crew would claim that after silencing the six-pound guns on the island with return shot from their carronades, the crew of the *Finch* pushed four carronades overboard in an attempt to lighten it and drift the vessel off the rocks. The records of Macdonough's prize master indicate that all guns were accounted for at capture; the crew of the *Finch* had, however, jettisoned 2,500 pounds of its powder supply. The powder was recovered by American crews shortly after the battle.

The gunboats that accompanied the *Finch* immediately turned northwest and challenged the *Ticonderoga*; they were repulsed by her superior firepower: Lieutenant Cassin had the *Ticonderoga*'s guns loaded with grapeshot. The shower of small round shot raked the decks of the approaching gunboats, leaving their crews scrambling for cover. Although Downie had ordered the gunboats' crews to board and seize the American vessels, no credible reference has been found for a claim that the British boarded any of the American vessels. British court-martial testimony indicates that no British gunboat approached close enough to an American vessel to attempt a boarding.[6]

By 10:30 a.m., the *Eagle*'s starboard spring line had been severed by enemy fire, and its bow began to swing west in the current. Its starboard guns were rendered ineffective and its aft deck exposed to a raking shot by the British brig *Linnet*. Henley ordered the best bower cable and the other spring cut, causing the ship to wind west and drift south in the current behind the *Saratoga* to a position between the *Saratoga* and the *Ticonderoga*. He anchored with a fresh larboard broadside, the port guns, now facing the British *Confiance*. Although the effect of the move was ultimately an advantage in Macdonough's contest with the *Confiance*, the *Saratoga* was left exposed to the *Linnet*'s guns while the *Eagle* moved. Macdonough was annoyed. Had the *Eagle* reanchored any closer north, Macdonough's ability to wind ship would have been jeopardized. Luckily, Henley's new position left enough open water for the *Saratoga* to maneuver.[7]

About fifteen minutes later, with the *Saratoga*'s starboard guns dismounted or damaged, Macdonough ordered the ship's crew to standby. Following Macdonough's orders, Sailing Master Brum carried the crew through the

"*Close Action.*" Master Commandant Thomas Macdonough at Plattsburgh Bay, 11:35 a.m., September 11, 1814. Dean Mosher, 2002. *War of 1812 Museum, Battle of Plattsburgh Association. Used with permission.*

winding maneuver: "A stern anchor was let go, the bower cable cut, and the ship winded with a fresh broadside on the enemy's ship." With seven of his ship's original broadside guns disabled and seeing the *Saratoga* winding, Robertson gave the order to wind the *Confiance* as well. Without a reliable complement of anchor set, the task could not be achieved, and his vessel sat unable to maneuver and at the mercy of the American flagship.

The combined fire of the two fresh broadsides was too destructive. The *Saratoga's* full larboard broadside is said to have carried the *Confiance's* masts "by the board." The fore main, mizzen and bowsprit were severely damaged; their condition later being described as "all shiver'd to Pieces." The spanker and jib booms were shot away, two-round shot pounded through the galley and, as noted, the ship's gigs were destroyed. With the American ships out of range of the British shore guns, the British gunboats almost totally ineffective, the *Chubb* and *Finch* disabled and the *Confiance* now facing the fresh guns of the *Saratoga* and the *Eagle*, the contest had taken a concluding turn. From the renewed fire of the *Saratoga*, one shot smashed a seven-foot hole in the *Confiance* planking below the water line; it began to list dangerously to starboard. To keep it afloat, the crew began to move as much of the ship's weight to port, bringing the damaged planking just above the water line. Cooper notes that Downie had "miscalculated his own powers of endurance." Lieutenant Robertson of the *Confiance* wrote of the conditions:

> *Mr. W. Martin and his assistant Mr. A. Todd all the time being unremitting in their attention to the unfortunate Sufferers: the latter was wounded by a Splinter, and a woman attending him was killed by the side of the Surgeon; The numerous wounded below were frequently moved from place to place to prevent their being drowned, though the utmost exertions were made by Mr. Cox, the Carpenter; who during the Action drove in sixteen large Shot plugs under the water line. Having to contend with such distressing circumstances, I joined in the opinion with the remaining Officers that while making no longer resistance it would be the height of in-humanity any longer to expose the lives of the unfortunate wounded.*

Unlike the suspect statement attributed to the dying former lieutenant Joseph Smith, Lieutenant Robertson's statement bears notice. The naval capture list indicates that three women were among those taken from the British ships; they were noted as "a woman, a woman, a woman"—no names. As there were four major British vessels, can we assume that there was, indeed, a fourth woman, and that she died?

Listing and taking on water below decks, the crew of the *Confiance* furiously pumped and bailed to keep the rising water from consuming the wounded lying about the lower deck, all the while shifting whatever they could to the port side. With guns disabled, ability to maneuver destroyed, a major part of the crew killed or injured and the ship sinking, Robertson saw the situation as grave. Robertson had 3,460 rounds and a seemingly endless supply of powder remaining (over 11,000 pounds) at this point, but the situation was hopeless. He ordered his vessel's colors stuck; the *Confiance* was surrendered at 10:50 a.m. Judge Hubbel would later remember the sight on the deck of the British flagship: "Here was a horrible sight. The vessel was absolutely torn to pieces; the decks were strewed with mutilated bodies lying in all directions, and everything was covered with blood."

With the *Confiance* out of the action, Macdonough turned the *Saratoga*'s guns on what was left of the *Linnet* and its twelve-pounders: a listing, almost defenseless hulk. The *Linnet*'s main yards and jib boom were reduced to broken timbers, its sails and rigging cut and ship's boats destroyed. As with the *Confiance*, although it had significant quantities of shot and powder remaining (1,750 rounds and 4,500 pounds of powder), the crew was now busy protecting what was left of it. The rising water in its belly was a foot above the bottom deck, and it was now being battered by the fresh thirty-two- and forty-two-pound carronade broadside of the *Saratoga*. Seeing the futility of continued struggle, its colors were ordered struck.

At 10:54 a.m., the thundering exchange on the lake turned silent. The naval conflict concluded with the wafting smoke of the *Saratoga*'s last broadside and the cries of the wounded. The British navy surrendered its beaten major vessels as their gunboats made for the open waters of the lake. Once in the broad lake, the battle-weary British gunboat crews could rest and let the lake's current carry them northward. The prize inventory showed that even after over two hours of battle, the British fleet's residual powder weighed seventeen thousand pounds. Macdonough would later describe the achievement as a "signal victory" in his report to the secretary of the navy.[8]

On land, with the exception of the right battery within range of

The British navy surrender. *From Panel 5, City of Plattsburgh Heritage Trail. Lee Hunt, 1993. Used with permission.*

the guns from Fort Moreau, the British artillery and rocket batteries were mostly undamaged throughout the day. Major John Suth Sinclair reported to General Baynes after the battle:

> *Our Battery most to the Right being by no means completed, and exposed to an Overpowering and in some degree plunging fire within 700 yards of the Enemy's numerous and heavy Artillery mounted on his Redoubts, was unable long to keep up a brisk fire, and when I visited that Battery soon after it had opened, I found the fire on it so heavy, that I directed Captain Gordon who commanded it, not to Attract the Enemy's attention, but reserve his Fire, until he should perceive our Troops advancing to the Assault, which support from this Battery would most materially have favored, all the enemy's Guns being in Barbette and the more to distract the Enemy's Fire I placed a Light Half Brigade in an advantageous situation about 600 yards to its Left and rear, which had a considerable effect in doing so; Soon after, however, the Carriges of both the Light 24 Pounders being considerable wounded, and several Men disabled, I directed Captain Gordon to place his Men under cover, and retire his Guns behind the Merlons, until circumstances should admit of using them to greater advantage.*[9]

With the vessels on the lake in full engagement, at 10:00 a.m. the major British land force set off from Power's encampment on the West Road southward on Hammond's Road. The route quickly dissolved into a series of logging roadways as it approached the Saranac River. Referring to the actions that followed, Lucas correctly states, "It is not easy to understand from the conflicting accounts what actually happened." In Robinson's words:

> *The troops placed under my command for the attack of the enemy's works consisted of the demi-brigade of the First Brigade (3rd Battalion 27th and 76th regiment). The 3rd Brigade, under Maj.-Gen. Power, consisting of the Buffs, 5th, 1st Battalion 27th, and 58th regiments, also the Light Companies of the 29th and 88th regiments, a brigade of six-pounders under Major Green—two only of which advanced—and two squadrons of the 19th Light Dragoons. A rocket detachment, and two or three wagons followed loaded with such ladders as I had been able to collect in the farm houses. The column was led by the eight light companies under the command of Brevet Lieut.-Colonel Lindsay, of the 39th, and the whole proceeded for Pike's Ford, under the guidance of the Quartermaster-General's department...*

The Saranac, at Pike's Ford, is about seventy yards wide, from two to three feet deep, with broad slippery stones at the bottom, and tolerably rapid. When we had nearly reached the ford on advancing, we heard three cheers from the Plattsburg side. I then sent Major Cochrane to ascertain the cause. Having marched nearly a mile and a half, the road branched off into a number of cart roads into a thick wood, and the officers of the Quartermaster-General's department were divided in opinion whether we were on the right road or not. Major Thorn, Assistant Quartermaster-General to my brigade, came to me and assured me we were wrong, and that he would undertake to conduct to Pike's Ford, without fear of any further mistake. We accordingly retraced our steps, and in about an hour we arrived on the banks of the Saranac. The wood was very thick on our side to within a few yards of the bank, which was about 60 or 70 feet high and very steep. I ordered the head of the column to halt in order to close up the light companies for a rush through the river. The light companies of the 3rd Battalion, 27th and the 88th, were posted to cover the rest while crossing. The men then advanced under a galling fire from about 400 of the enemy posted behind trees and bushes, and rushed through the ford, with an impetuosity that nothing could check. They were supported by the 3rd Battalion, 27th, under Major Mills, in gallant style—the light companies pursuing the enemy till they had reached the ground they were ordered to occupy. The 76th regiment followed and formed in column about half a mile on the opposite side of the ford; the two six-pounders were let down the bank by large detachments, and the 58th Regiment crossed and formed in column in rear of the 76th.

British captain Mackenzie Kennedy of the Seventy-sixth Regiment recalled the march to the Saranac: "They were conducted by a circuitous route, by the guide, to a ford of the Saranac, which though very deep, they succeeded in crossing without much opposition by the enemy."

Robinson's after-battle journal entries indicate his frustration with Prevost's leadership: "It appears to me that the army moved against Plattsburg without any regularly digested plan." He referred to Wellington's intelligence tactics in Spain, gathering information as to the "exact" location of the most suitable passages across the river Bidassoa in northern Spain, the officers subsequently leading the columns directly to the most advantageous ford. There had been no similar initiative under Prevost, and little, if any, emphasis on intelligence gathering.

The overland route to Pike's former encampment was unknown to the British, and there is no indication that Prevost actively sought to determine the size of the American force that opposed him. The battalions had crossed the river and formed a column of approximately one mile on the roadway leading south toward the Salmon River settlement, the roadway that had been cleared for them by the Macomb's nighttime landscape gardeners. Fitz-Enz posits that Power's force met the militia "formed up for battle in straight lines" in an open field. Perhaps he was speaking of the encampment's small parade ground, but quite the contrary situation existed, according to Ransom Cook. He speaks of the trees being twenty to thirty feet high and in full foliage on the lands beside the roadway. It would not have been possible to see for any distance. Fitz-Enz speaks of the American militia being dislodged and retreating south, "where perhaps they could make a stand." In accordance with Macomb's instructions, the New York militia offered a token challenge from the woods on the western side of the roadway as the British column pressed on—a strategic retreat.

From Robinson's own words (which follow shortly), we know that the militia did as it had been instructed by General Macomb; the men fired from behind the trees and rocks as they withdrew toward the settlement. Ransom Cook speaks of the British continuing their advance after the militia, "determined to rush into the forts pell mell with them." Cook's account continued, "The British, not doubting but the militia were taking the shortest route to the forts at the mouth of the river, rushed after them."

The Vermont militia occupied the eastern side of the roadway. It had been ordered not to fire until it heard the American cannons from the Salmon River settlement. Macomb's anticipation of the British flanking route had been correct.

Preparations for their reception had paid off. The militia forces of New York and Vermont performed as Macomb instructed, leading the British column south to the Salmon River settlement "amid the bushes on the five mile road to the American Stores."[10]

Robinson states:

> *The 1st Battalion, 27th, had nearly crossed, when I rode forward to give the necessary directions for the attack. I had hardly reached the front, when Major Cochrane came and delivered to me the order for retiring... the "Confiance" and the brig [Linnet] having struck their colours in consequence of the frigate having grounded, it will no longer be prudent to persevere in the service committed to your charge, and it is therefore the orders of the Commander of the Forces that you immediately return with the troops under your command...I communicated this to Maj.-Gen. Power;*

who was equally astonished with me at the contents, and lamented the cause of the order. The whole immediately retired under cover of the light companies, and the two six-pounders posted on the bank.

The only accident that happened was to the 76th Light Company, owing to too great zeal and daring in Captain Purchase, who, conceiving it possible to take a gun from the enemy, did not obey the order for retiring, in consequence of which about twenty-five men, with himself and two subalterns, were intercepted. Captain Purchase was killed with eight or ten of the men, and the remainder were taken prisoners…The enemy made a slight attempt to follow us, but retired as soon as they came within reach of the six-pounders. The whole of the troops returned to their former ground and, in the course of the evening, orders were given for the Army to retire.

Baynes issued orders for the First Battalion to return to Chamblee and LaPrairie; the Second to LaColle, Isle aux Noix and St. Johns; and the Third to Odelltown.

Documentation shows that the British column did not halt within a short distance from the rear of the works and remain until the naval engagement concluded (as frequently stated); it was under march when it was surprised by the lack of noise from the lake and the muzzle blast from cannons in front of the column.

Robinson's journal entry explains that his column stretched out over a mile south beyond the river and recounts the efforts of the Seventy-sixth in trying to capture a cannon. The only documented locations of American cannons outside the village on September 11 were as directed by Macomb at Crab Island and at the Salmon River settlement, the two there entrusted to Lieutenant Sumpter near the headquarters of General Mooers and the bridge crossing the Salmon River. The settlement was located over a mile due south of the ford at Pike's Cantonment and a mile west of the lake. Robinson did later claim that he had been within such close range of the American positions "near the bridge" that he could see their uniforms. The local newspaper account of the action west of the village recounts the movements of the major British ground force and corroborates their being south and about a mile and a half west of where Prevost expected them to be:

The enemy attempted at the same time to throw his main body in rear of the fort, by crossing the river three miles west of the town, near the site of Pike's cantonment. He succeeded in crossing after a brave resistance by the Essex militia and a few of the Vermont Volunteers, in all about 330 stationed at that place, who retired back a mile and a half from the river, continually pouring in upon them an incessant fire from behind every tree, until lieutenant Sumpter brought up a piece of artillery to their support, when the enemy commenced a precipitate retreat. The Vermont Volunteers, who had hastened to the scene of action on the first alarm fell upon the enemy's left flank and succeeded in making many prisoners, including three officers.

Robinson wrote of the morning's encounter: "The men then advanced under a galling fire from about 400 of the enemy posted behind trees and bushes...The only accident that happened...The enemy made a slight attempt to follow us, but retired as soon as they came within reach of the six-pounders."[11]

It would appear that the British had been successfully drawn south toward Lieutenant Sumpter's cannons and the troops stationed at Mooers's headquarters near the bridge at the Salmon River settlement. Macomb's orders dictated that if an advancing column could not be stopped, the supplies there were to be destroyed. The militia forces had pulled the British into a pocket of small-arms fire from a mostly unseen force of unknown size on both flanks (New York militia on the west and Vermont militia on the east). The Americans were leading the advancing British column into the path of American cannon muzzle. The invading column, formed in the open on the roadway, was the target for those hidden behind the rocks and trees. This new form of engagement, today called "guerilla warfare," was recognized some thirty years later by Major John Richardson, a British veteran of the campaign in the Americas, as a disadvantage when fighting the Americans:

Accustomed to the use of the rifle from his infancy—dwelling in a measure amid forests with the intricacies of which he is wholly acquainted, and possessing the advantage of a dress which renders him almost undistinguishable to the eye of a European, the American marksman enters with comparative security into a contest with the English soldier whose glaring habiliment and accoutrements are objects too conspicuous to be missed, while his utter ignorance of a mode of warfare, in which courage and discipline are of no avail, renders the struggle for mastery even more unequal.

Robinson would years later express a similar feeling, remarking that Americans don't fight like gentlemen but rather from behind rocks and trees. Prevost, from atop the Allen House on the northern side of the river, waited for his column to come from the west. He waited...and waited. The sudden silence on the lake would have enabled Prevost to hear the far-off small-arms and cannon reports from an area he knew was too far south and west of where Robinson should have been. The rising smoke would provide the realization that Robinson's column was engaged and nowhere near the American fortifications.

The situation must have heightened Prevost's sense of alarm: Why are they to the west? What's happening? Are they surrounded? Were Bathurst's expressed cautions present in Prevost's decision to recall the ground force? He would later report to Bathurst of being deprived "of the cooperation of the fleet without which the further Prosecution of the Service was become impracticable...the most complete success would have been unavailing, and the possession of the Enemy's Works offered no advantage to compensate for the loss we must have sustained in acquiring possession of them."

Christie spoke of the American foe as having "numerous reinforcements which momently crouded in," giving to Macomb "a great disposeable force, whose superiority in numbers was such that a delay of a few hours might have placed the British in a critical situation." George Stanley notes that Prevost, believing that the fate of his assault was most affected by the defeat of the navy, missed completely the fact that there were so few casualties in the land skirmishes. Where was the great and superior force south of the Saranac River? Had Macomb grown his numbers in the eyes of the British commanders with the aid of smoke and mirrors?[12]

Macdonough described the condition of the vessels on the lake:

> *There was not a mast in either squadron that could stand to make sail on; the lower rigging, being nearly all shot away, hung down as though it had been just placed over the mast heads. The* Saratoga *had fifty-five rounds shot in her hull; the* Confiance *one hundred and five. The enemy's shot passed principally just over our heads, as there were not twenty whole hammocks in the nettings at the close of the action, which lasted, without intermission, two hours and twenty minutes.*

Lieutenant Henley of the *Eagle* reported, "31 round shot in our hull (mostly 24-pounders), four in our lower masts, and we were well peppered with grape."

There is a much-repeated reliance on Macdonough's September 11, 1814 after-battle letter to Secretary Jones when describing the damage to the British vessels. The numbers of hull shot that Macdonough reported to Jones on that day were preliminary, however, and did not reveal the true extent of the damage to the vessels. The reports to Macdonough from the prize masters appointed by him to assess the damages reveal the sobering truth of the ferocity of the event. Daniel Records, assigned as the *Confiance* prize master, reported "from 250 to 300 Cannon Shot in the Hull, and Grape without number." Damages for each of the smaller British vessels revealed their similarly grave condition: *Linnet*, thirty to fifty hull shots; *Chubb*, thirty-four hull shots; and *Finch*, five ("three of which under water"). The British fleet had taken a true pounding from the American guns; this is, perhaps, a tribute to Macdonough's insistence on pre-battle gunnery practice. The Plattsburgh paper (years later) stated that "winter clothing for the whole of the land army" was aboard the British fleet. The prize masters' inventories of the stores aboard the British ships show only six hundred suits of sailors' clothing.[13]

As noted, the British galleys turned to and withdrew into the broad lake beyond Cumberland Head. The winds, still from the north but lessened, would have made their escape restful if not for the American gunboats in pursuit. Further engagement was averted by the need for damage control; the major vessels were seriously damaged. Macdonough recalled, "When all the vessels were reported to me to be in a sinking state; it then became necessary to annul the signal to the galleys, and order their men to the pumps." The escaping British gunboats were then free to coast northward in the lake current, their crews no doubt contemplating the disastrous event in which they had been participants.[14]

After the return of the British column from south of the Saranac, Prevost's force began as orderly a retreat as could be achieved. Eleazer Williams tells of the British batteries firing throughout the day and into the evening, stopping at nine o'clock. Williams himself was wounded in the last cannonades of the day. While the American forces enjoyed a brief respite from the action, across the Saranac, the march to the border had been going on since noon, and the British now began to remove their guns as rainfall came.

Throughout the rainy night and into the next morning, they worked to disassemble their batteries. The lack of sufficient wagons and carts, and the poor condition of the crude roadways (the significant downpour rendering them mud-clogged) frustrated their efforts. While all of the guns were removed and successfully transported back to Canada, those stores and ordnance that could be destroyed or dumped without consequence were disposed of. In the light of the assumed British victory and apparent winter occupation plans, the baggage, stores, munitions and ordnance buildup from the sixth to the eleventh was so significant that the means for immediate withdrawal did not exist; indeed, they were not planned for. Major Sinclair of the Royal Artillery reported to General Baynes that fifty thousand cartridges and all of the remaining twelve-pound shot were destroyed, in addition to any other shot or shells for which transport could not be arranged.

Describing the lack of transportation and conditions, Sinclair wrote:

> *For want of means of Transport, which became necessarily inadequate to the removal of the whole at once from the increased proportion of Guns, Ammunition & Stores which had been brought up, from the Rear by such means as we were in possession of, and which could not be augmented by any recources [sic] to be found in the Enemy's Country. Several Wagons & Carts from being Overloaded (in order to remove as much as possible) and the extreme badness of the Roads broke down, leaving no alternative but to destroy them and their Contents. The Ammunition, stores &c placed in Depots in Rear being situated on Lake Champlain were nearly all embarked in Sloops, Bateaux &c and withdrawn. At little Chazy about 50 shells were thrown into the Lake and I am informed that a Sloop laden with Stores (partly Ordnance Stores) unfortunately sank off Isle la Mothe [sic] and fell into the hands of the Enemy.*

Macdonough later reported to Secretary Jones that "about six tons of 9 inch shells" were recovered. General Macomb described the British activity in leaving:

> *At night moved off his heavy baggage and under the darkness retreated with his whole army towards Canada leaving his wounded on the field and a vast quantity of Bread, flour and Beef which he had not time to destroy, besides a quantity of bomb shells, shot, flints and ammunition of all kinds, which remain at the batteries and intrenching tools of all sorts, also tents and marquees. A great deal was found concealed in ponds and creeks, and buried in the ground, and a vast quantity carried out by the inhabitants.*[15]

On the morning of the twelfth, it was apparent that the British had withdrawn. Macomb ordered regulars and militia to follow the British retreat, taking prisoners and deserters and returning with the wounded and sick. Williams's journal describes the conditions:

> *The rain had been pouring down with such torrents during the night, as to put the road into such a state as to become almost impassable. It had*

The Battles at Plattsburgh (September 11, 1814)

General Macomb's map. *From* U.S. Air Force National Register Evaluation of Archaeological Sites *[at]* Plattsburgh.

been passed over, during the night, by more than four hundred carts of the enemy, besides the battering train of artillery, so that by twelve o'clock, our progress had been but eight miles. The cavalry, riflemen, and light infantry were several hours in advance, while we were thus drudging in a road, with mud sometimes almost up to our knees, gun after gun stuck and upset in the quagmire, and the horses were staggering and reeling under their burdens.

Macomb ordered the pursuit to end and began his after-action report to the secretary of war; he included his sketched map of the battlefield.

Under a flag of truce, Prevost sent a letter to Macomb requesting information regarding the wounded and killed and humane treatment of the wounded and sick. Macomb replied positively and promised to forward details resulting from the naval battle. Macdonough's sailors busied themselves with repairing their vessels, keeping the British vessels afloat and tending to the wounded.[16]

The numbers of wounded from the naval battle were significant. Macomb and Macdonough ordered the sick and wounded, both American and British, to the field hospital established on Crab Island. All were treated with courtesy and compassion. The kindness of Macomb in his treatment of the captured was saluted in the *London Times*. The treatment of the wounded British by the American surgeons and attendants was noted by the British officers in letters of thanks to Macdonough and their reports to their superiors:

> *I have much Satisfaction in making you acquainted with the humane treatment the wounded have received from Commodore McDonogh. They were immediately removed to his own Hospital on Crab Island, and were furnished with every requisite. His generous and polite attention also to myself, the Officers and Men, will ever hereafter be gratefully remembered. (Lieut. Robertson,* Confiance*)*

The numbers of wounded and sick soon overwhelmed the resources and staff of the island hospital. In the village, the white Shaker nuns, living in a spacious Bellevue Street (now Cumberland Avenue) home owned by Henry DeLord, cared as they could for the wounded and sick of both sides. Macdonough paroled sixty of the injured and sick prisoners, removing them to the British hospital on Isle aux Noix.

The exact number of those British killed on the lake was, and remains, difficult to establish. The *London Gazette* carried an initial summary of naval killed (57) and wounded (72) in November 1814, but as they noted, without the ability to muster and not knowing the number of bodies lost during battle, the numbers remain only an estimate. The American naval personnel killed and wounded were first listed in the *American State Papers* in 1834. For the *Confiance*, Robertson reported 38 bodies but could not determine the exact number of killed, as bodies had been thrown overboard in clearing the deck as the action continued. Macomb told his father that 115 Americans had been killed and 130 wounded in the land battle on the eleventh. From Fort Moreau on the twelfth, John Rochester described to his father the previous day's "constant firing of cannon, shells, bombs & rockets," which continued all day, and the loss of "one man killed and 2 wounded by a rocket." Macomb would later describe the rockets as doing little harm: "More frightful than dangerous." Prevost wrote to Bathurst of the land casualties: 37 killed, 150 wounded and 57 missing. The Dorsetshire Regiment history indicates 13 killed, 10 "left sick in America" and 28 captured as prisoners by the Americans.[17]

On Crab Island, the dead of both combatants were buried. Simeon Doty told of seeing

> *trenches dug, ranging from north to south into which the bodies were placed. Some of them were rolled up into blankets and others had only their ordinary*

clothing on. Their heads were placed to the west and their faces downward. The Americans and British were buried indiscriminately together.

The graves on the southern part of the island were unmarked and remain that way today, the location known to but a few. The names of those interred there were first published in the *Plattsburg Republican* in 1903.[18]

George Beale Jr., Macdonough's purser, compiled a listing of killed and wounded from the American fleet:

Return of killed and wounded on board the U.S. Squadron on Lake Champlain, in the engagement with the British Fleet, on the 11th of September, 1814.

SHIP SARATOGA
Killed
Peter Gamble, lieutenant.
Thomas Butler, quarter gunner.
James Norberry, boatswain's mate.
Abraham Davis, quarter master.
William Wyer, sail maker.
William Brickell, seaman.
Peter Johnson, do.
John Coleman, do.
Benjamin Burrill, ordinary seaman.
Andrew Parmlee, do.
Peter Post, seaman.
David Bennett, do.
Ebenezer Johnson, do.
Joseph Couch, landsman.
Thomas Stephens, seaman.
Randall McDonald, ordinary seaman.
John White, do.
Samuel Smith, seaman.
Thomas Malony, ordinary seaman.
Andrew Nelson, seaman.
John Sellack, do.
Peter Hanson, do.
Jacob Laraway, do.
Edward Moore, do.

Jerome Williams, ordinary seaman.
James Carlisle, marine.
John Smart, seaman.
Earl Hannemon, seaman.
Total, 28.

WOUNDED
James M. Baldwin, acting midshipman.
Joseph Barron, pilot.
Robert Gary, quarter gunner.
George Cassin, quarter master.
John Hollingsworth, seaman.
Thomas Robinson, do.
Purnall Smith, do.
John Ottiwell, do.
John Thompson, ordinary seaman.
William Tabee, do.
William Williams, do.
John Roberson, seaman.
John Towns, landsman.
John Shays, seaman.
John S. Hammond, do.
James Barlow, do.
James Nagle, ordinary seaman.
John Lanman, seaman.
Peter Colberg, do.
William Newton, ordinary seaman.
Neil J. Heidmont, seaman.
James Steward, do.
John Adams, landsman.
Charles Ratche, seaman.
Benjamin Jackson, marine.
Jesse Vanhorn, do.
Joseph Ketter, do.
Samuel Pearson, do.
Total, 19 [sic].

BRIG EAGLE
Killed
Peter Vandermere, *master's mate.*
John Ribero, *seaman.*
Jacob Lindman, *do.*
Perkins Moore, *ordinary seaman.*
James Winship, *do.*
Thomas Anwright, *do.*
Nace Wilson, *do.*
Thomas Lewis, *boy.*
John Wallace, *marine.*
Joseph Heaton, *do.*
Robert Stratton, *do.*
James M. Hale, *musician.*
John Wood, *do.*
Total, 13.

Wounded
Joseph Smith, *lieutenant.*
William A. Spencer, *acting lieutenant.*
Francis Breeze, *master's mate.*
Abraham Walters, *pilot.*
William C. Allen, *quarter master.*
James Duick, *quarter gunner.*
Andrew McEwen, *seaman.*
Zebediah Concklin, *do.*
Joseph Valentine, *do.*
Joseph Hartley, *do.*
John Miclin, *do.*
Robert Buckley, *do.*
Aaron Fitzgerald, *boy.*
Purnell Boice, *ordinary seaman.*
John N. Craig, *seaman.*
John McKenney, *do.*
Matthew Scriver, *marine.*
George Mainwaring, *do.*
Henry Jones, *do.*
John McCarty, *do.*
Total, 20.

SCHOONER TICONDEROGA
Killed
John Stansbury, lieutenant.
John Fisher, boatswain's mate.
John Atkinson, do.
Henry Johnson, seaman.
Deodrick Think, marine.
John Sharp, do.
Total, 6.

Wounded
Patrick Cassin, seaman.
Ezekiel Goud, do.
Samuel Sawyer, do.
William LeCount, do.
Henry Collins, do.
John Condon, marine.
Total, 6.

SLOOP PREBLE
Killed
Rogers Carter, acting sailing master.
Joseph Rowe, boatswain's mate.

Wounded
None

GUNBOAT BORER
Killed
Arthur W. Smith. Purser's steward.
Thomas Gill, boy.
James Day, marine.

Wounded
Ebenezer Cobb, corporal marines.

GUNBOAT CENTIPEDE
James Taylor, landsman, wounded.

The Battles at Plattsburgh (September 11, 1814)

GUNBOAT WILMER
Peter Frank, seaman, wounded.

GUNBOATS
Nettle, Allen, Viper, Burrows, Ludlow, Alwyn, Ballard,---
none killed or wounded

RECAPITULATION

	Killed	Wounded
Saratoga,	28	29
Eagle,	13	20
Ticonderoga,	6	6
Preble,	2	0
Borer,	3	1
Centipede,	0	1
Wilmer,	0	1
	----	----
	52	58

Approved: T. Macdonough.
George Beale, Jr., Purser.

The foregoing listing, together with other listings relating to the naval battle, was published years later in the *American State Papers*.[19]

The *London Times* reported fifty-seven deaths and seventy-two wounded from among the officers and crew of the British fleet:

A Return of the Killed and Wounded on board His Majesty's late Squadron, in Action with the Enemy's Squadron on Lake Champlain, 11ᵗʰ September 1814

Confiance—*3 officers, 38 seamen and marines, killed;*
1 officer, 39 seamen and marines, wounded.
Linnet—*2 officers, 8 seamen, killed;*
1 officer, 13 seamen and marines, wounded.
Chub—*6 seamen and marines killed;*
1 officer, 15 seamen and marines, wounded.
Finch—*2 seamen and marines wounded.*
Total—129.

From the Confiance's *crew having been landed immediately after the action, no opportunity has offered a muster. The number stated is the whole as yet ascertained to have been killed and wounded.*
Names of the Officers killed and wounded
Killed
Confiance
George Downie, Captain
Alexander Anderson, Captain of Royal Marines.
William Gunn, midshipman.
Linnet
William Paul, acting lieutenant
Charles Jackson, boatswain.
Wounded
Confiance
------ *Lee, midshipman*
Linnet
John Sinclair, midshipman
Chub
James M'Ghee, lieutenant

Macdonough would later confirm that among the 1,050 members of the British fleet, there had been 84 deaths and 110 wounded among the captured.[20]

The *London Times* informed the British public that members of the British fleet had been transferred to the American installation at Greenbush or paroled:

> *Capt. D. Pring, on parole; Lieutenants Hicks, Creswick, Robinson, M'Ghie, Drew, Hornsby, Childs, lieutenant marines, and Fitzpatrick, lieutenant 39th Regiment; Sailing Master Bryden; Masters' Mates Clark and Simmonds; Surgeon Todd; Purser Gile; Captain's Clerk Guy; Midshipmen Dowell, Aire, Bondell, Toorke, Kewstra; Davidson, boatswain; Elvin, gunner; Mickell, gunner; Cox, carpenter; Parker, purser; Martin, surgeon; M'Cabe, assistant surgeon. 47 wounded men paroled.*[21]

A complete listing of the 343 British crew members (including the 3 women) and their officers captured on the lake appears with the "1812–1814 Stations to Lake Champlain."[22]

The militia and volunteers were dismissed by General Mooers on September 13. With the thanks of Generals Macomb and Mooers, General Strong and the Vermont volunteers began the return to their state.

The Battles at Plattsburgh (September 11, 1814)

The *London Times* reported the sentiment of Burlington's citizens as printed in their local paper: "The ringing of bells, discharges of musketry, and salute's of ordnance from the wharf and encampment, proclaimed the joy of our citizens, and their gratitude to their heroic deliverers." Macomb and Macdonough generally complimented the forces in their reports to the secretaries of war and the navy, respectively. Their letters have been widely addressed by various authors through the years.[23]

Macdonough and Robert Henley of the *Eagle* started the process of seeking transfers from Lake Champlain, Macdonough to seek a new battle fleet command and Henley, apparently, to escape Macdonough's control. Henley, not receiving an acknowledgement of his transfer request, again wrote to Macdonough. We know that Macdonough was not pleased with Henley's performance aboard the *Eagle*, was annoyed with Henley's prior interference in the naming of the vessel, distrusted Henley's after-battle report of sick and injured and was apparently wary of Henley's sudden claims of sickness. In the draft of a letter to Elisha Winter written later in October, Macdonough speaks of his disappointment with Henley's conduct. He wrote, "I shall always say that Lt. Henley did his duty," but in an apparent afterthought, he struck the sentence from the letter. Macdonough may have "sat" on Henley's requests for transfer. A frustrated Henley resigned command of the *Eagle* on September 17 because of "health reasons," leaving for Burlington on the eighteenth.[24]

In assessing the achievements of Macdonough and Macomb at Plattsburgh, Allan Everest summed up their performance by stating that "these two young men deserve more nearly equal honor. They complemented each other, and in the battle of Plattsburgh, each might have met a different fate without each other."[25]

On September 14, as crews of the American fleet attended to the repairs of the damaged vessels of both sides, fallen officers of both fleets were removed to the shore. A long procession of military and civilians accompanied the dead to their burial place in the village cemetery: foes in battle, equals in death. From his quarters aboard the *Saratoga*, Macdonough began the somber task of writing to the families of the fallen American officers: "It becomes my painful duty…"[26]

With the reports from his officers, Macdonough was able to complete a report of the force size and losses from both sides:

RECORD OF THE FORCE AND LOSS OF THE AMERICAN AND BRITISH FLEETS

AMERICAN

	Guns	Men	Killed	Wounded
Saratoga, ship	26	210	26	20
Eagle, brig	20	120	13	27
Ticonderoga, schooner	17	110	6	6
Preble, sloop	7	30	1	1
10 Gunboats	16	350	3	3
	----	----	----	----
Totals	86	820	49	57

The American officers killed were Lieutenants Gamble and Stansbury, and Sailing Master Carter.

ENGLISH

	Guns	Men	Killed	Wounded
Large ship,	39	300	50	60
Brig,	16	120	20	30
Sloop, formerly Growler,	11	40	6	10
Sloop, formerly Eagle,	11	40	8	10
11 Gunboats,	16	550	2	
3 probably sunk*	----	----	----	----
Totals	93	1050	84	110

The British officers killed were Commodore Downie, Captain Pring and six or eight lieutenants. The wounded were paroled and sent by vessel to the Isle aux Noix.

*Eleazer Williams also indicated that some British galleys were destroyed; no confirming data exists for the statement.[27]

The returns of General De Rottenburg, published in the *London Gazette* in late November 1814, reveal the impact of the actions on the British land forces:

> *Return of Killed, Wounded, and Missing of the Left Division, under the Command of Major-General de Rottenburg, in Action with the Enemy, from the 6th to the 14th September 1814…*
>
> *Total—2 captains, 1 ensign, 4 serjeants [sic], 30 rank and file, 1 horse, killed; 1 general staff, 1 captain, 6 lieutenants, 7 serjeants, 135 rank and file, 2 horses, wounded; 4 lieutenants, 2 serjeants, 1 drummer, 48 rank and file, 6 horses, missing.*

Names of Officers. Killed—
3ᵈ Foot—Captain (Brevet Lieutenant-Colonel)
James Willington, Ensign John Chapman.
76 Foot—Captain John Purchase.
Wounded—General Staff—Captain T. Crosse, Aide-de-Camp to Major-
General De Rottenburg, slightly.
3d Foot—Lieutenant R. Kingsbury, severely (since dead); Lieutenant*
John West, severely; Lieutenants G. Benson and John Home, slightly;
58 Foot—Captain L. Westropp, severely; Lieutenant C. Brohier, slightly;
Lieutenant and Adjutant-Lewis, slightly.
Missing—76 Foot—Lieutenants G. Hatch, G. Ogilvie, and E.
Marchington;
Canadian Chasseurs—Lieutenant E. Vigneau.(Sgd) Edw. Baynes, Adj.
Gen. N.A.

*Lieutenant Kingsbury, Third Buffs, died on the morning of September 10.[28]

The Buffs reported killed 3 officers (Willington, Chapman, Kingsbury), 4 drummers and 30 rank and file. Their wounded were 3 officers, the first sergeant, 7 Sergeants and 135 rank and file; missing were 4 officers, 2 sergeants and 49 rank and file. The Fifty-eighth Northhamptonshire Regiment's records show "4 men killed, 3 officers, 1 sergeant, and 29 men wounded."[29]

In the Chesapeake, after the attack on Washington, General Ross was killed at the battle of North Point on the twelfth.

Inhabitants of the village of Plattsburgh began the return to their homes and businesses. Peter Sailly started the chore of collecting the remains of the military provisions that had been transferred to the forts before the battle. He reported that a large portion of the flour had been damaged. The *Montreal Herald* carried news of the defeat on September 17: "It must afford a sad tale in the page of British history…we must now instantly redouble our energies to obtain the command of the Lake, or with humility await our future destiny." Macomb issued orders to suspend the sale of "spirituous liquors" to the military and, two days later, finding that the soldiers were "idling their time about the streets" and alternately schlepping to the village "tippling shops," declared the establishments off limits, tightening the requirements for the issue of passes. He ordered the building of barracks, quarters, a hospital and store buildings close to the forts. To prevent price gouging, he empowered the inspectors general to regulate the price of all items offered for sale to his soldiers.[30]

Even as repairs were being made to the damaged vessels and bodies were still washing up on the shore of Lake Champlain, a public dinner was held to celebrate the victory and importance of the battle.[31]

From Montreal, Prevost wrote to Bathurst on September 22:

> *The disastrous and unlooked for result of the Naval Contest by depriving me of the only means by which I could avail myself of any advantage I might gain, rendered a perseverance in the attack of the Enemy's position highly imprudent, as well as hazardous. From the state of the roads Each days delay at Plattsburg made my retreat more difficult. The Enemy's Militia was raising En Masse around me, desertion increasing & the Supply of Provisions Scanty. Excluded from the advantage of water conveyance, & that by roads passing through Woods & over Swamps becoming, from the State of the weather as well as from the obstructions made by the Enemy nearly impassable. Under the circumstances I had to determine whether I should consider my own Fame by gratifying the Ardor of the Troops in persevering in the Attack, or consult with more substantial interests of my Country by withdrawing the Army which was yet uncrippled for the security of these Provinces.*
>
> *The most ample success on shore after the loss of the Flotilla could not have justified the sacrifice I must have made to obtain it. Had I failed, & such an event was possible after the American Army had been cheered by the sight of a Naval Victory, the destruction of a great part of my Troops must have been the consequence, & with the remainder I should have had to make a precipitate and embarrassed retreat, one very different from that which I have made. These are considerations, which without doubt will have their own due weight with Your Lordship, & induce you, I trust, to view the measures I have adopted, as those best calculated to promote, as well, the honor of His Majesty's Arms, as the safety of this part of his Dominions.[32]*

On September 24, the American naval crews were still employed in the repair and maintenance of their vessels (and the captures) and dragging for anchors lost on the eleventh. The British left Isle La Motte, but a brigade remained at Champlain guarding the remaining pieces of artillery, which, because of the condition of the roads, could not yet be removed. On the twenty-ninth, prize inventories and necessary repairs completed, the British vessels were in a condition that enabled their removal to Whitehall. Macdonough reported to Secretary Jones that, in accordance with Jones's request, 550 men were in readiness to proceed to Sackets Harbor if needed.[33]

The Battles at Plattsburgh (September 11, 1814)

A significant chapter in American history ended with the mundane tasks of recovery, the mop-up activities that follow conflict, heroism, pain and sorrow. To appreciate history is to learn from the past. Vigilance and intelligence-gathering are both art and skill. Those closest to Plattsburgh's situation recognized the threat and proposed the correct course of action in response. The American government's highest military and civilian leaders were made aware of the growing British strength in Canada and the planned invasion. Warnings and warning signs were ignored. If not for the resourceful management and military skills of two young officers, Macdonough and Macomb, what would have been the outcome? What would have been our history? What have we learned?

8

Aftermath

I found many interesting items that resulted from or followed the events at Plattsburgh; a few are presented here.

Izard was sensitized by criticisms of his move from Plattsburgh before the invasion and what he felt was a building perception that he had left the forces there in a disadvantaged state. He reminded Secretary of War Monroe of the orders that had been given him by Monroe's predecessor and requested that the secretary apprise the president of the state of readiness and capabilities of the officers left in charge of Plattsburgh. He ended, "I am anxious to prove that I have not been undeserving of the confidence, which has been placed in my exertions, to defend the frontier entrusted to my charge."[1]

Macdonough continued to enjoy the praise of the public and the government he served. In the first week of October, Secretary of the Navy William Jones wrote to the Naval Committee of the Senate about the naval victory on Lake Champlain, "It is perhaps one of the most important events in the history of our country."

Even in the shower of praise, Macdonough had to suffer the embarrassment of not being able to pay the navy's bills. On October 12, he was invited to a dinner given in his honor at Waterford, New York, but on the same day he wrote to John Bullus, the New York navy agent:

> *I am in a singularly bad situation on this Lake, no person will cash a draft because as they say it will not be paid. The apothecaries have refused medicines to the surgeon for the sick, and we suffer other serious inconveniences from the same cause of disbelief among the inhabitants that the draughts will be paid.*[2]

"Macdonough's Medal." *From* Harper's Encyclopedia of United States History.

By mid-October, with winter approaching and discounting a new lake invasion by the British, Macdonough ordered most of the American fleet to Whitehall and again requested a transfer. He wrote to Secretary Jones, "As Naval operations are considered at an end on this lake, I beg you will be pleased to release me in this command." There was a bit of concern when it was later reported that enemy boats were landing at Chazy. Detachments of the Sixth and Twenty-ninth Regiments were sent north. They discovered that a few British gunboats made an appearance but had withdrawn. The naval activities subsided as Macdonough had believed they would. The remainder of the British fleet moved into the Sorrel River to escape the coming winter ice. The month ended with Macdonough preparing for the same and anticipating an early November move to Whitehall, the winter home of the Lake Champlain fleet.

On land, Macomb remained in command at Plattsburgh; to the north, Brisbane commanded at St. Johns. British major general Edward Pakenham was appointed by the prince regent to replace the fallen General Ross. There must have been some confusion on the part of Bathurst who addressed his letters to the army officer as "Sir T. Pakenham." "Sir T." was, perhaps, a reference to Thomas Pakenham, a Royal Navy admiral. Edward Michael Pakenham, the army officer, was the brother-in-law of Lord Wellington and had served with "the Duke" in Portugal.[3]

Peter Sailly continued the task of gathering and accounting for the military provisions at Plattsburgh. He reported the state of stores to Macomb: "About

"Macomb's Medal." *From* Harper's Encyclopedia of United States History.

100,000 rations of pork and about 116,000 rations of beef, in all 216[,000] rations of meat, which will last 72 days if issued at the rate of 3,000 rations per day. The flour will about hold out with the meat. The supply of whisky will not last more than 35 days." It appeared that all was getting back to normal. Sailly returned to the task of stopping the black market trade with the British and requested payment for his fences; his neighbor, Nathaniel Platt sought payment for the loss of his wharf and storehouse. Macomb, now promoted by the president to major general, was focused on the daily business and discipline of the military. The courts-martial resulting from the previous months found six men guilty of desertion; they were shot to death on the twenty-eighth.[4]

General Pakenham, in the Chesapeake, was to continue with Bathurst's diversionary plan by attacking the American coast as he moved southward and, after being sent more forces, to enter the Gulf and attack New Orleans. He was to proceed against New Orleans even if he heard that "preliminaries of Peace between His Majesty and the United States have been signed in Europe" and was instructed against "exposing the troops to hazard or serious loss for an inconsiderable advantage." New Orleans was a disappointing end to the British plan for the end of the conflict with the United States.[5]

The post-battle stature of the two American commanders continued to climb. In London, their matter-of-fact reports of the Plattsburgh battles drew notice in the *London Times*:

Aftermath

Written in a plain manly style, with very little appearance of exaggeration, and with none of that violent and vulgar abuse of the English, by which many American officers have not ineffectually courted the favors of their own Government.[6]

The *Confiance* was dismasted and its deck covered to make it a floating barracks. The lake's American naval crews moved in to weather the winter cold and, in the boredom of a winter in "ordinary," to wait for their share of the prize money resulting from the capture of the British fleet. As the wheels of their government moved in customary slow motion, the crews' displeasure steeped in the damp cold about them. George Beale, Macdonough's former purser and, later, the government's prize agent, wrote to Macdonough (now in Middletown, Connecticut) of the conditions and discontent. "Sailors, you know, are not reasonable beings," he mused, referring to the crew's impatience with the lack of payment. Some of the crew, their naval commitment fulfilled, sold their future prize distribution for half the expected amount. Beale begged Macdonough for his help in securing a new assignment.[7]

Macdonough would later become a rich man by the prize money. In 1818, Beale certified the distribution of the $266,711.17 in prize money:[8]

Commodore McDonough $22,807.00
Lieutenant command't Stephen Cassin 4,552.25
Lieutenant (9), Sailing Master (11) 2,012.75
Lieutenant marines (1) 1,443.20
Steward (8), Coxswain (1), Surgeon's Mate (3),
Midshipman (18), Armorer (1), Botswain's
Mate (3), Carpenter's Mate (1),
Master-at-arms (1) 1,427.13
Surgeon (2), Chaplain (1), Boatswain (3),
Gunner (2), Master's Mate (15), Sail-maker (1),
Purser (1) 1,163.62
Seaman (247), Ordinary Seaman (204),
Landsman (21), Boy (20), Private (177) 120.42
Quartermaster (8), Quartermaster's Mate (1),
Quarter-gunner (21), Pilot (4), Corporal (4),
Sergeant (3), Musician (1) 668.10

The end of the year concluded with the release of Lieutenant Smith and others who had been captured by the British on the lake in June 1813, the announcement that Macomb had been named by the War Department to command the northern frontier and the signing of the treaty for peace on Christmas Eve.[9]

Macdonough would subsequently command at Portsmouth Navy Yard and, years later, after several other assignments, aboard the USS *Constitution*. He died in late 1825 on his return trip to the United States after relinquishing command of the *Constitution* in the Mediterranean.

George M'Glassin, who led the midnight raid against the British battery, moved to Philadelphia and became the publisher of the *National & Commercial Gazette* after an 1818 court-martial and being cashiered out of the military for "unnecessarily and cruelly whipping soldiers, of his company."[10]

Eleazer Williams, whose service had become so necessary during a period of war, found himself suddenly unnecessary to his former government employer. He was left fighting for pension rights into 1816, seeking the aid of General Mooers in securing help through Governor Tompkins's office to bolster his case with Washington's bureaucracy:

> *Will you be so good as to represent our case to Mr. Adgate. If you should find among your papers General Dearborns Letter to you, which I was the bearer, dated sometime in the month of August 1812* [a reference to the Aug 6, 1812 letter from Dearborn to Mooers; see note 13 in chapter 2] *you will enclose the same to the Lieut. Governour. I think, If I can obtain that Letter it will render us an essential service at Washington.*[11]

A year after the engagements at Plattsburgh, Henry DeLord leased the Bellevue Street house in which the nuns had cared for some of the wounded after the battle. Among the lease clauses, he added, "And women of bad quality shall not dwell in said building." Interpretation of this remark escapes me.[12]

George Prevost would be called to England to face a court-martial; the four charges were:

- *that Prevost had induced Downie to attack by leading him to expect the co-operation of the land forces, and had not given that cooperation;*
- *that he had not stormed the American works on shore at the same time that the naval action began, as he had given Downie to expect;*
- *that he had disregarded the signal for co-operation, which had previously been agreed upon;*
- *that he had not made a land attack either during or after the naval action, whereas, if he had done so, the squadron might have been saved.*

Aftermath

Prevost died on January 5, 1816, at the age of forty-eight, before having the opportunity to defend himself. Of Prevost's performance in the Americas, it has been said, "His instructions and temperament made him cautious to a fault." Prevost's brother, Colonel William Augustus Prevost, and Lady Catherine Ann Prevost petitioned for the favor of the prince regent upon the memory of Sir George and his long and distinguished career in the service of the Crown. Eventually, the prince regent did publicly and favorably acknowledge the accomplishments and service of Sir George, but the public ridicule and defense continued for years.[13]

In their reports of the action, Macomb and Mooers praised Captain Aikin's Rifle Company for its usefulness and bravery. Macomb had promised each of the volunteers a rifle as a "reward for their gallant and meritorious conduct." The Rifle Company waited until 1822 for recognition and another four years before, by congressional resolution in 1826, each received his rifle. A Hall Model 1824 breech-loading rifle with a personalized silver commemorative plaque and thumb shield was given to each surviving member of the company, the rifles having been made at Harpers Ferry, West Virginia.[14]

Caleb Nichols invoiced the government for the use of his island and damages to his property; his $615 bill included a charge of $150 for burying 150 men on his island.[15]

The British army contracted for nineteen thousand cords of wood to warm the troops encamped in Lower Canada for the coming winter, enough that if stacked cord-to-cord, they would stretch for more than twenty-eight miles.[16]

Appendix I
Plattsburgh with the "H"

The property where the city of Plattsburgh sits today was given to Zephaniah Platt by Governor Clinton, the first governor of the state of New York, during the years 1784 to 1787. The governor gave the 30,000 acres of land by executing (signing) several documents commonly referred to as land grants. Grants are frequently not easy gifts. There was a requirement that a settlement be established on the land within seven years. Mr. Platt worked fast, and in 1785, a settlement had been established and a government organized, and the "Township of Plattsburgh," with the "h," was officially recognized by a special act of the legislature of the state of New York. One of the original land grant documents survives and is stored in the archives of the city. The document, dated February 28, 1787, is one of the last given to Mr. Platt. The document conditionally transferred 1,320 acres to the west of the established boundaries of the town of Plattsburgh to Platt.

In 1797, the first post office was established in the area. The official name given to the post office was "Plattsburgh," the name taken from the official designation of the town as given by the legislature of the state.

In 1815, the area surrounding the Cumberland Bay had become heavily populated. Because of the protection of the bay and its location at the mouth of the Saranac River, shops and mills were being established, docks had been built and the area had become a port of trade on Lake Champlain. There was a need for a more local government, close to the thriving port. On March 3, 1815, the village of Plattsburgh was incorporated within the boundaries of the town of Plattsburgh. Note that the spelling of both names is identical: with the "h."

In 1859, the village was reorganized (without changing the spelling of the name). In 1902, the village, seeing more advantages under the laws of the state for its citizens, was reorganized and chartered as the city of Plattsburgh. The official minutes of the village and, now, the city of Plattsburgh are recorded in large volumes stored in the city archives.

Close to the end of the year 1950, the editor of the *New York State Legislative Manual*, seeking to simplify the organization of that year's manual, requested a listing of state post offices from the U.S. Postal Service. Upon review of the listing, the difference in spelling was noted. The city was contacted, and an investigation was begun by postal authorities. U.S. Postal Service records show that the name of the local *post office* was changed to "Plattsburg," without the "h," in 1894.

During the period from 1892 to 1894, the federal Post Office Department was growing at a rapid pace. The postmaster general issued an order establishing guidelines for post office names for new post offices. The order was misunderstood by local postal officials, who caused the name of the village *post office* to be changed to "Plattsburg," without the "h." As a result of the 1951 investigation, the name of the city *post office* was changed back to "Plattsburgh," with the "h."

At no time was the spelling of the name of Plattsburgh, the municipal entity, ever changed.

.

Appendix II
Bathurst's "Secret" Orders

To: General Ross
Copy
Downing Street, Secret
20ᵗʰ. May 1814.
Sir

It having been judged expedient to effect a diversion on the Coast of the United States of America in favour of the Army employed in the defence of Upper & Lower Canada; Admiral Sir A. Cochrane has received Instructions to direct a Squadron to proceed with a detachment of Troops and a Battalion of Marines towards those places on the Coast where it may appear to him most advisable that a descent should be made; and H.R.H. the Prince Regent confiding in your valour, enterprize, and discretion, has been graciously pleased to commit to you the command of these Troops in such operations as you may judge it expedient when on shore to undertake—

In addition to the force which may have been placed under your orders previous to your departure from the Gironde, you will on your arrival at Bermuda, take under your command one other Regiment of Infantry & one Company of Artillery which have been directed to proceed thither from the Mediterranean for that purpose—

The amount of the force which will be thus placed under your command (& which is specified in the margin) will sufficiently point out to you that you are not to engage in any extended operations at a distance from the Coast—

In concerting the particular object of attack with the Officer in command of the naval part of the Expedition, you will express to him your opinion of its expediency in a military point of view, and will without reserve state the difficulties or facilities with which its execution may be attended. You will also consider yourself authorized to decline engaging in any operation which you have reason to apprehend will lead from the probability of its failure to the discredit of the Troops under your command, or will expose then to a loss disproportioned to the advantage which it may be the object of the attack to attain—

While afloat you will consider yourself as under the command of the Naval Officer commanding this Expedition—The disembarkation of the Troops and their reembarkation will be directed by him; but he will be instructed to concert with you as to the best mode of effecting the same respectively—You will decide as to the time when you may consider it expedient to reembark the Troops, as that must in a great degree be regulated by the success of your undertaking, and by the approach of the Enemy's Force, but you will previously ascertain whether in the opinion of the Commander of the Naval Force there is any period positively unfavourable for reembarkation—

You will regularly transmit to me for the information of H.M. Government detailed Accounts of your proceedings & of any operations in which you may have been engaged—

When the object of the descent which you may make on the Coast is to take possession of any Naval or Military Stores, you will not delay the destruction of them in preference to the taking them away, if there is reasonable ground of apprehension that the Enemy is advancing with superior force to effect their recovery.

If in any descent you shall be enabled to take such a position as to threaten the Inhabitants with the destruction of their property, you are hereby authorized to levy upon them contributions in return for your forbearance, but you will not by this understand that the Magazines belonging to the Government, or their Harbours, or their Shipping are to be included in such arrangements; These together with their contents are in all cases to be taken away or destroyed.

You will not encourage any disposition which may be manifested by the Negroes to rise upon their masters—The humanity which ever influences H.R.H. must make him anxious to protest against a system of warfare which must be attended by the atrocities inseparable from commotions of such a description. If however any individual Negroes shall in the course of your operations join you or give you assistance, & if you have reason to believe that they would in consequence be exposed to the vengeance of their masters after your retreat, you are at liberty on their earnest desire to take them away with you, and you are authorized, if they are willing to enlist, to enlist them in any of the Black Corps; but if they evince no such disposition, you will consign them to the care of the Admiral commanding who has received instructions as to their disposal—But you must distinctly understand that you are in no case to take slaves away as slaves, but as free persons not subject to any restrictions incompatible with the state of free persons.

I have &c
Bathurst[1]

To: General Prevost
Secret
Downing Street,
3rd June, 1814.
Sir,
I have already communicated to you in my dispatch of the 14th of April the intention of His Majesty's Government to avail themselves of the favourable state of Affairs in Europe, in order to reinforce the Army under your command. I have now to acquaint you with the arrangements which have been made in consequence, and to point out to you the views with which His Majesty's Government have made so considerable an augmentation of the Army in Canada.

[R.&F. 768] The 4th Battalion of the Royal Scots of the strength stated in the margin sailed from Spithead on the 9th ulto. direct for Quebec, and was joined at Cork by the 97th Regiment destined to relieve the Nova Scotia Fencibles at Newfoundland; which latter will immediately proceed to Quebec.

[R.&F. 6th 980, 82.837] The 6th and 82nd Regiments of the strength as per margin sailed from Bordeaux on the 15th ulto. Direct for Quebec. Orders have also been given for embarking at the same port, twelve of the most effective Regiments of the Army under the Duke of Wellington together with three Companies of Artillery on the same service. This force, which (when joined by the detachments about to proceed from this Country) will not fall far short of ten thousand infantry, will proceed in three divisions to Quebec. The first of these divisions will be embarked immediately, the second a week after the first and the third as soon as the means of Transport are collected. The last division however will arrive at Quebec long before the close of the year. Six other Regiments have also been detached

*from the Gironde and the Mediterranean, four of which are destined to be
employed in a direct operation against the Enemy's Coast, and the other
two are intended as a reinforcement to Nova Scotia and New Brunswick;
available (if circumstances appear to you to render it necessary) for the
defence of Canada, or for the offensive operations on the Frontier, to which
your attention will be particularly directed. It is also in contemplation at a
later period of the year to make a more serious attack on some part of the
Coasts of the United States; and with this view a considerable force will
be collected at Cork without delay. These operations will not fail to effect a
powerful diversion in your favor.*

[R.&F. 3127] *The result of this arrangement, as far as you are
immediately concerned, will be to place at your disposal the Royals, The
Nova Scotia Fencibles, the 6th & 82nd Regiments amounting to three thousand
one hundred and twenty seven men: and to afford you in the course of the
year a further reinforcement of ten thousand British Troops. When this force
shall have been placed under your command, His Majesty's Government
conceive that the Canadas will not only be protected for the time against any
attack which the enemy may have the means of making, but it will enable
you to commence offensive operations on the Enemy's Frontier before the close
of this Campaign. At the same time it is by no means the intention of His
Majesty's Government to encourage such forward movements into the Interior
of the American Territory as might commit the safety of the Force placed
under your command. The object of your operations will be; first, to give
immediate protection: secondly, to obtain if possible ultimate security to His
Majesty's Possessions in America. The entire destruction of Sackets harbour
and the Naval Establishments on Lake Erie and Lake Champlain come
under the first description. The maintenance of Fort Niagara and so much
of the adjacent Territory as may be deemed necessary: and the occupation
of Detroit and the Michigan Country come under the second. If our success
shall enable us to terminate the war by the retention of the Fort of Niagara,
and the restoration of Detroit and the whole of the Michigan Country to
the Indians, the British Frontier will be materially improved. Should there
be any advanced position on that part of our frontier which extends towards
Lake Champlain, the occupation of which would materially tend to the
security of the Province, you will if you deem it expedient expel the Enemy
from it, and occupy it by detachments of the Troops under your command,
always however taking care not to expose His Majesty's Forces to being cut
off by too extended a line of advance. If you should not consider it necessary
to call to your assistance the two Regiments which are to proceed in the first*

instance to Halifax, Sir J. Sherbroke will receive instructions to occupy so much of the District of Maine as will secure an uninterrupted intercourse between Halifax and Quebec. In contemplation of the increased force which by this arrangement you will be under the necessity of maintaining in the Province direction have been given for shipping immediately for Quebec, provisions for ten thousand men for six months. The Frigate which conveys this letter has also on board one hundred thousand pounds in Specie for the use of the Army under your command. An equal sum will also be embarked on board the Ship of War which may be appointed to convoy to Quebec the fleet which is expected to sail from this Country on the 10th or at the latest on the 15th instant.

I have the Honor etc.,
Bathurst[2]

<hr />

To: General Pakenham
London 24th Octr 1814
M. Genl. The Hon
Sir T. Pakenham
Sir:
The Prince Regent having been pleased to confer upon you the Command of all the Troops operating with His Majesty's Fleets upon the Coasts of the United States of America, I have received His Royal Highness' Commands to desire that you would proceed forthwith to join Sir Alexander Cochrane, and to assume the command of the Forces which are ordered to assemble at a fixed point of Rendezvous.

The troops which have been employed in the Chesapeake under the late Major General Ross are the 41st, 44th and 85th Regiments with two Companies of Artillery. A strong Body of Marines has been incorporated with that Division.

The 93rd Regiment, part of the 95 Rifle Corps, a company of Artillery and a Corps of Sappers and Miners together with a Squadron of the dismounted Light Dragoons under the orders of Major General Keane sailed from England last month, and will probably unite with the former Corps in the latter end of November. The Command of the whole will dissolve upon Major General Keane, who will be reinforced at the same time by the 5th West India Regiment and 200 Black Pioneers.

It is probable that this force will have proceeded from the approximated Rendezvous before your arrival there, in order to carry into execution the Plans contemplated by Sir Alexander Cochrane.

You will be followed immediately by the 7th and 43rd Regiments with another squadron of dismounted Dragoons, which are embarked at Plymouth under Major General Lambert, and by the—Regiment from Cork. The 2nd West India Regiment has also been ordered to join you from Barbadoes.

I enclose herewith for your information copies of all Instructions which have been addressed to Major General Ross, Keane and Lambert. Those to General Ross explain so fully the views and Intentions of His Majesty's Government that I consider it unnecessary to do more than request your attention to the points upon which these instructions bear, and your adherence to the Principles which are there laid down.

I am persuaded that you will preserve the best understanding between the Military and Naval Forces of His Majesty employed upon this service; and I beg to assure you that you possess the full confidence of His Majesty's Government, and that you may rely upon any constant support and upon the readiest attention being paid to your ideas and suggestions.

I have etc
Bathurst[3]

To: General Pakenham

Downing Street 24th Octr 1814
M Genl
Sir T. Pakenham
Secret
Sir,
In my instructions to Major General Ross of the 6th September, I explained the conduct which it would be fit to pursue, if the inhabitants of New Orleans and part adjacent should be disposed to take an open part against the Government of the United States, either with a view of establishing their own Independence, or of again placing themselves under the Spanish Government.

As you are not however authorized to enter into any Engagements on the part of Great Britain on this subject, it is not perhaps to be expected that the Inhabitants will be willing to take any active part against a Government to which on the Signature of a Peace between Great Britain and the United States, they might afterwards be obliged to submit, but it is probable that a general disposition may exist, peaceably to acquiesce in our Possession of the Country during the War.

You will give every encouragement to such a Disposition; and you will for that purpose cause the force under your command, to observe the strictest Discipline; to respect the Lives and the Property of all those inclined to a peaceable deportment and by no means to excite the Black Population to rise against their Masters. There is nothing so calculated to unite the Inhabitants against you as an attempt of this description, while the apprehension of your being obliged to resort to such a measure for your own protection may be made to act as an additional inducement with them to make no resistance to His Majesty's Forces.

I have etc
Bathurst[4]

⟫⋅⟪

To: General Pakenham
War Department
24th October 1814
M Genl The Hon
Sir T. Pakenham
Secret
Sir:
It has occurred to me that one case may arise affecting your situation upon the Coasts of America for which the Instructions addressed to the late Major General Ross have not provided.

You may possibly hear whilst engaged in active operations that the Preliminaries of Peace between His Majesty and the United States have been signed in Europe and that they have been sent to America in order to receive the Ratification of The President.

As the Treaty would not be binding until it shall have received such Ratification in which we may be disappointed by the refusal of the Government of the United States, it is advisable that Hostilities should not be suspended until you shall have official information that The President has actually ratified the Treaty and a Person will be duly authorized to apprise you of this event.

As during this interval, judging from the experience we have had, the termination of the war must be considered as doubtful, you will regulate your proceedings accordingly, neither omitting an opportunity of obtaining signal success, nor exposing the troops to hazard or serious loss for an inconsiderable advantage. And you will take special care not so to act under the expectation of hearing that the Treaty of Peace has been ratified, as to endanger the safety of His Majesty's Forces, should that expectation be unhappily disappointed.

I have etc.
Bathurst[5]

Notes

ABBREVIATIONS

BM: Bailey-Moores Collection
BP: Bloomfield-Pike Letterbook
JMSI: Journal of the Military Service Institute
JRUSI: Journal of the Royal United Service Institution
PR: Plattsburgh Republican
PRO: Public Record Office
NA: National Archives
NAC: National Archives of Canada
NHC: Naval Historical Center
USN: United States Navy

INTRODUCTION

1. While there may be several contemporary writings and websites still stating that the location of Pike's encampment is disputed, the U.S. government has recognized the documentary and archaeological findings fixing the location near Fredenburgh Falls on the south side of the Saranac River; the site is now recognized as National Historical Register eligible (see Herkalo, *Antiquarian & United States Air Force*). The archaeological investigation of the site in 2011 yielded military artifacts directly attributable to Pike's Fifteenth Infantry.
2. Louisiana State University, "Statistical Summary"; Nordhaus, "American Casualties"; Heinrichs, "The Losers," 51; Warren to Melville, November 18, 1812; Warren to Melville, February 25, 1813.
3. Muller, *Proudest Day*, 339, cites data from the 1933 Vermont State document (State of Vermont, *Roster of Vermonters*, 459) detailing Vermont citizens who

served in the War of 1812. Vermont's Eleazer Williams is shown to have served in Stearn's company of volunteers and to have been at the Battle of Plattsburgh.

CHAPTER 1

1. Brackenridge, *History of Late War*, 21; Naval Historical Center, *Documentary History*, vol. 1, 29–31; Phillips, *James Fenimore Cooper*, 60; Whitehill, *Cooper as Naval Historian*, 468–79.
2. Ansley, *Vergennes*, 202; PR, March 31, 1900, 1c2, Business on Lake Champlain in 1811:

> *The value of exports from the District of Champlain, for the months of May and June of this year* [1811] *was $296,914. Among them were 1327 bbls. pork, 160 bbls. cider, 4918 bushels corn, 20,386 lbs. butter, 7,330 lbs. hogs lard, 25,880 lbs. candles, 31,630 lbs. leather, 100 tons potash, 13, 700 lbs. soap, and also large quantities of tea, tobacco, tallow, boots and shoes, &c. Forty-three rafts were cleared during these months containing 1,253,000 cubic feet of pine lumber, principally Norway; 195,080 cubic feet oak timber; 1013 spars; 20,500 pairs staves; 2800 ash oars, and 700 walnut handspikes, valued in the aggregate at $181,279.00.*

3. *PR*, November 1, 1811, 3c2–4.
4. See Everest, *War of 1812*, 38.
5. *PR*, November 15, 1811, 3c1–3.
6. NHC, vol. 1, 60; Skeen, *Citizen Soldiers*, 12.
7. *PR*, December 20, 1811, 3c1–2; Everest, *War of 1812*, 42.
8. *PR*, December 1811, 3c4.
9. Skeen, *Citizen Soldiers*, 19–21.

CHAPTER 2

1. Everest, *War of 1812*, 47.
2. USN RG45, Area File 7. Daniel Tompkins to John Bullus, July 13.
3. Tuttle, *Three Centuries*, 165.
4. Ibid., 192.
5. NA (M148), roll 10, June 1, 1812, to December 31, 1812, item 67; Middletown, June 26, 1812, letter to Honorable Paul Hamilton, secretary of the navy: "Sir, The United States now [aiming?] at War. I solicit your order for service in the Navy and hope you will favour me with such a situation as in your opinion I am suited to hold."

6. Benn, *Iroquois in the War*, 36; *PR*, July 17, 1812, 2c4, 3c1.
7. Bixby, "Peter Sailly," 77. Sailly to the secretary of the treasury, July 27, 1812.
8. BM, Box 17, Folder 233. Dearborn to M.G. Benjamin Moores:

> *Head Quarters Green Bush, July 29ᵗʰ 1812—You will please to procure a suitable character for obtaining information from day to day, or as often as practicable, of the movements of the enemy. The amount of his force at each post un Upper Canada,—taking care to distinguish between regular forces & militia; to ascertain what additional force has arrived at Quebec this season;—what number have been moved from Quebec to Montreal & its vicinity;—what sort of works are constructing at different points; whether any measures are in operation with the enemy for providing any floating force on the Lake, & what appears to be the general disposition of the Inhabitants of Canada, including the Indians in relation to the war. Some confidential, intelligent person should be employed for obtaining correct information on these points, & suitable encouragement given him. You will please to consult Mr. Saillie, the Collector on this subject; & take his advice in relation to the selection of a suitable person for the above purposes. You will please to forward, by the mail, via Burlington to this place the information as soon as obtained. Every possible precaution & discretion should be used for keeping the names of the persons employed, a profound secret—whether they be citizens of the U. States—or Subjects of the enemy. If any important information should be obtained, that may require a more certain, speedy, or confidential conveyance, than the mail—an express, that can be relied on for integrity & celerity of movement should be dispatched. I hold myself accountable for all necessary expenses, attending the measures, which I have here directed;—& money will be supplied from time to time for that purpose. No offensive operations should be commenced on your part until further orders but every exertion should be used to resist any attempts of the enemy on your posts, or on the territory of the U. States.*

9. *PR*, December 1886, 1c4–5. It is interesting to note that Muller, who places Williams's position and importance in a more or less proper perspective, misidentifies Williams's origin. (Muller notes, 339 [see F-1]—"Records show that Eleazer [also called Lazar, Lazare, Lazarre, Lazo] Williams volunteered for the war from Bakersfield, Vermont. He held pension certificate No. 30391," info that was gleaned from the *Roster of Soldiers*, 459: "WILLIAMS, ELEAZER, Bakersfield. Served in Capt. Stearn's company. Volunteered and was at the battle of Plattsburgh Sept. 11, 1814. Pension Certificate No. 30391.")
10. Hastings, *Public Papers*, 3:677–678. See also Lewis, "Plattsburgh's Veteran Exempts."

11. *PR*, July 31, 1812, 2c4:

The Veteran Exempts having set an example to the young men of the country, in the terms of their Association and offers of service, which have been accepted by his Excellency the Governor, and Brevets according to their choice issued to the men who are to command them. It becomes them now to organize, to uniform and equip—It is expected they will make choice of the most economical dress; that they will at the next meeting appear with their own arms, the Government not having as yet, provided any for them. And that they appear under their own standard. It is proposed that it be a black ground with 13 stars for the Union of White, wrought in silver. That in the center of the Flag there be a Death's Head, with cross bones under, intimating what is not seen, according to the course of nature, be their promiscuous fair, and the immediate one of any enemy who shall venture to contend with them—Under these an open wreath with this motto, "Thy will be done."

Over the Death's Head, surmounted as a crest, a Rattle-Snake with Thirteen rattles, coiled, ready to strike, with this motto in a similar wreath inverted over it. "Don't tread on me." It is the rule in Heraldry that the worthy properties of the crest borne shall be considered, and the base ones cannot be intended. The ancients recounted a Snake or Serpent an emblem of Wisdom. And in certain attitudes, of endless duration. The Rattle-Snake is properly a representative of America, as this animal is found in no other part of the world. The eye exceeds in brightness any other animal, so it indicates penetration. It has no eye lids, and is therefore an emblem of vigilance. It never begins an attack, nor ever surrenders—proofs of magnanimity and courage. When injured, it never wounds without giving its enemy notice of his danger. When in undisturbed peace, it does not appear to be furnished with any kind of weapons, they are hidden in its mouth, appearing, even when extended for defense to those who are not acquainted with them to be weak and contemptible, yet its wounds are decisive and fatal, certain destruction to its enemies. The power of fascination attributed to the Rattle-Snake, by a generous construction, resembles America. Those who look steadily on her are delegated and almost involuntarily advice towards her, and having once approached her never leave her. This Snake is often found with thirteen rattles, and they are said to increase yearly—It is beautiful in youth, and its beauty increases with its age. The exhibition of one with Nineteen Rattles, two thousand Miles long and its Head in the middle will astonish the Old World.

Miles Veteranus, July 29th, 1812

12. BM, Box 17, Folder 233. Dearborn to E Williams:

Head-quarters Greenbush August 5ᵗʰ, 1812—"For your services in the way proposed, I will engage to pay you at the rate of four hundred Dollars per year and allow you two rations per day; and for extra expences in traveling when necessary—And I will endeavour to afford you the means in the winter seasons for improving your Education—I shall expect the most perfect attention on your part to all directions as you may from time to time receive from me or from such General offices as I may find it proper occasionally to place you with. And most ridged punctuality & integrity will be indispensably necessary for you to observe as well as the greatest caution and prudence in relative to the business intrusted to your charge. Your accounts of necessary expences must be correctly kept and exhibited when required.

13. BM, Box 17, Folder 233. Dearborn to Major General Benjamin Moores

H.Q., Green Bush August 6ᵗʰ 1812—The Bearer, Mr. Williams, is on business for the Public, & if it should be necessary for him to go to St. Regis, you will please to have him furnished with a Horse. His business is of a confidential nature. He will consult you, & will wish to ascertain, where he can find old Co. Louis of the St. Regis Tribe, & whether you expect any of the Cochnawuga Chiefs at Plattsburgh soon; & whether you have any knowledge of his (Mr. Williams') Father, who is one of he Chiefs of that tribe. The most perfect secrecy must be preserved, in regard to this young man's business, name & connections. Any aid you can afford him will be desirable. His family have considerable influence with the Indians in your Neighborhood, & are desirous that the Indians in that quarter, may remain on neutral ground. If any of those people should be disposed to come within our lines, they should be treated in a friendly manner, & supplied with rations.

14. *PR*, December 11, 1886, 1c4–5.
15. Ibid.
16. Hanson, *Lost Prince*, 225.
17. *PR*, December 11, 1886, 1c4–5; BM, Box 6, Series 2; Mooers to Dearborn, August 22, 1812.
18. *PR*, December 11, 1886, 1c4–5.
19. Tuttle, *Three Centuries*, 276.
20. *PR*, September 11, 1812, 3c2.

21. Ibid., September 4, 1812, 2c1.

22. Ibid., December 11, 1886, 1c4–5; Tuttle, *Three Centuries*, 301.

23. *PR*, September 4, 1812, 2c1.

24. Ibid.

25. Tuttle, *Three Centuries*, 301.

26. *BP*, Bloomfield 37 and 40 to Secretary of War [Wm. Euestis], September 14, 1812.

27. Ibid., Bloomfield 42 to Dearborn, September 17, 1812; Myer, *Life and Letters*, 48.

28. *BP*, Bloomfield 52 to Winans.

29. Ibid., Bloomfield 58 to [H. Glen].

30. Ibid., Bloomfield 54 to Dearborn.

31. Fitz-Enz, *Final Invasion*, 29; County of Clinton City Maps. The winter site, Lot 66, Plattsburgh Old Patent (site of Pike's winter cantonment), was surveyed on October 10, 1811, by Pliney Moore/William Bailey and William Keese. See also Herkalo, "Location of Pike's Cantonment."

32. *BP*, Bloomfield 60 to Isaac Clark; Bloomfield 70 to Pliney Mooers, et al.

33. Everest, *War of 1812*, 87–101.

34. See *BP*, Bloomfield 64 to Captain Ducherman, September 22, 1812; Bloomfield 65 to Dearborn; Bloomfield 66 to Tompkins for details of payments and arrangements to those termed "expensive allies" by Bloomfield.

35. *BP*, Bloomfield 68 to Dearborn.

36. Ibid., Bloomfield 78 to Abner.

37. Ibid., Bloomfield 68 to Hatch.

38. Ibid., Bloomfield 70 to V. Goodrich.

39. Ibid., Bloomfield 69 to Petit; Bloomfield 73 to B.G. Petit.

40. Ibid., Bloomfield 72 to Major Sheridan.

41. Ibid., Bloomfield 74 to Tompkins.

42. Ibid., Bloomfield 81 orders. ("Cock," as used here, is assumed to be the shortened form of "Cochnawauga," an Anglo-phonetic spelling of the tribal name.)

43. *BP*, Bloomfield 83 to Dearborn.

44. Ibid., Memoranda, 2; Bloomfield 10 to Dearborn; 92 to quartermaster, French Mills.

45. Mann, *Medical Sketches*, 15.

46. *BP*, Bloomfield 55 to Dearborn.

47. Ibid., Memoranda, 2; Bloomfield 99 to James Madison; Bloomfield 109 to Dearborn; Bloomfield 120 to Wm. Billings.

48. Ibid., Bloomfield 87 to V. Goodrich; Bloomfield 10 to Dearborn; NA (M148), Roll 10, June 1, 1812, to December 31, 1812, item 83; *BP*, Bloomfield 113 to Ormes.

49. *PR*, December 11, 1886, 1c4–5.

50. Hanson, *Lost Prince*, 227–28; *BP*, Bloomfield 110 to Major White Youngs; *PR*, December 18, 1886, 1c3–4.

51. *BP*, Bloomfield 88 Orders; Bloomfield 97 to Thomas H. Cushing.

52. Tuttle, *Three Centuries*, 334; NA (M148), Roll 10, June 1, 1812, to December 31, 1812, item 107, item 124.
53. *PR*, October 23, 1812, 1c3.
54. *BP*, Bloomfield 103 to Dearborn; 104 to Jonas Galusha; 107 to Gen Ormes; 109 to Dearborn.
55. Ibid., Bloomfield 121 to Major Youngs comdg. St Regis; *PR*, December 1886, 1c3–4; *BP*, Bloomfield 123 to Martingdale.
56. Hanson, *Lost Prince*, 229. November 20, 1812:

> *A Council of War was held to-day, in which I appeared somewhat conspicuous, as I was the only person who could give the information desired. In the Council disclosures were made, to a certain extent in relation to the campaign, which were contrary to my expectations, and far from being honorable to the public service. Still there is hope for a revision of the decision of this council, and this must be upon certain circumstances in regard to the enemy, but in the meantime, every demonstration must be made by the American army of its intended invasion of the British Province. By the reports of the Rangers, the enemy is not so formidable in our front as to give any fears of the unfavorable result if our advance was made upon them. The Canadians are still unwilling to bear arms against the Americans, since they had a skirmish with the royal troops at LaChine, in August last. They are forced into the service, and no dependence can be placed upon them.*

In paraphrasing this entry, the *Plattsburgh Republican* added the following note: "Note: At the latter end of November our corps being, however, always on the alert and making provision for every surprise, the artillery train moved towards Plattsburgh for winter quarters and I went to Charlotte in Vermont." *PR*, December 18, 1886, 1c3–4.

57. *PR*, July 23, 1887, 1c4; Everest, *War of 1812*, 92; Myer, *Life and Letters*, 50.
58. Hanson, *Lost Prince*, 229; Myer, *Life and Letters*, 51; BM, Box 8, Folder 118; NA (M148), Roll 10, June 1, 1812, to December 31, 1812, item 227, Macdonough to Hamilton, Shelbourne, December 20, 1812:

> *I have the honor to inform you that on the* $[12]^{th}$ *of this month I landed at this place in a secure harbour* [the] *U States vessels on this lake. The weather came so boisterous and the Ice making. Thought it imprudent to keep out lon*[ger] *one of the sloops (the* Growler, *commanded by Lt. Smith having a few days* [ago] *been dismasted in a squall—*[Mr.] *Loomis Sailing Master, Mr. Montieth Midshipman and Mr Beale Purser, have come on…Twenty two men from New York. I am* [get]*ting every thing in readiness for the spring and trust nothing will be wanting to* [?]

with the army when it gets in motion [?] then, to make these vessels as affective [as] they might be one hundred would be [?pany] which would be but a [?case] complement. The enemy has at the Isle au Noix their Gun Boats carrying, tis said, by several prisoners that have been there two twenty four pounders each, and fifty men. These sloops of about eighty [tons] mounting six six pounders, and a twenty [four] each with about fifty men on board each sloop, and lately, I have learned they are fitting out a schooner to mount twelve or fourteen guns, and told also [is manned however lean]…should be able to cope with them. The vessels that I now have are the Sloop President mounting six collumbiad & two long twelves—The Sloop Growler with two twelves and one long eighteen on a circle—The Sloop Eagle with six sixes and one eighteen on a circle—and two gun Boats carrying a long twelve each; you will observe that the other three sloops are for transport.

59. Everest, *War of 1812*, 95; Myer, *Life and Letters*, 52; Mann, *Medical Sketches*, 19, 45; *BP*, Pike 124 to General Chandler. Pike relates personnel strength at Plattsburgh to Chandler—800 + 474 + dead (200)=1,474—at Cantonment Saranac; *PR*, October 13, 1877, 1c3. Jeremiah Barnes speaks of seeing several hundred comfortable log houses.

60. Herkalo, "Location of Pike's Cantonment," 1.

CHAPTER 3

1. Hanson, *Lost Prince*, 230–32.
2. Ibid., 32.
3. NA (M148), Roll 11, January 2–June 30, 1813, item 16, item 20.
4. Hanson, *Lost Prince*, 233–34.
5. *BP*, Pike 10 to Dearborn, February 20, 1813; United States to Benjamen Moores, Dr. Paid Racoon (an Indian) and others for making snowshoes [on warrant of] Colonel Pike, $25 Receipt, Lilly Library.
6. *BP*, Pike 1 to Callender Irvine; Pike 2 to Dearborn; Pike 3 to Colonel Pierce; Pike 4 to Mooers.
7. Ibid., Pike 4 to Dearborn; Hanson, *Lost Prince*, 233.
8. Hanson, *Lost Prince*, 234; *BP*, Pike 10 to Dearborn; *PR*, March 15, 1812, 3c2; *BP*, Pike 13 to Colonel Pierce; Pike 15 to Ephraim Whitlock; Pike 16 to General Chandler; Pike 18 to Dearborn.
9. *BP*, Pike 126 to Dearborn; Pike 20 to first brigadier of the Northern Army; Pike 18 to General Woolsey.
10. Ibid., Pike 22 to General Chandler; Hanson, *Lost Prince*, 234; *BP*, Pike 23 to Major General Dearborn; Pike 32 to Woolsey; Pike 36 to Lieutenant Barnet,

15th Infantry; Pike 130 to Dearborn; Pike 135 to Major George Bomford; Pike 140 to John Armstrong.

11. Hanson, *Lost Prince*, 235–36; BM, Box 8, Folder 118, April 3, 1813, receipt: "US to John Stevenson, Dr. to board Eleazer Williams & Lewis Cook, Indian Chiefs from the 3th of April to the 19th 2 weeks and one day 12.85 May 10 boarding Eleazer Williams 4 days & boarding his horse $2.50 [and so on to July 4] $59.50 Certified by B.M. Acting Indian Agent by request of Genl. Dearborn."

12. Hanson, *Lost Prince*, 236; BM, Box 8, Folder 114, April 27, 1813, receipt: "Received of Benj Mooers Indian Agent ten dollars to account to him for the...also fifteen dollars for Solomon Talbourn & Louis Vondri...and also five dollars for Col. Louis Cook."

13. *PR*, April 30, 1813, 2c4; NA (M148), Roll 11, January 2–June 30, 1813, item 20, item 21.

14. *PR*, January 1, 1887, 1c8; Hanson, *Lost Prince*, 236–37; *PR*, June 4, 1813, 3c3.

15. Tuttle, *Three Centuries*, 153, 161–62; Hanson, *Lost Prince*, 237 (Williams's entry "Plattsburg, July[sic: June] 3, 1813, Note: The *PR* [January 1, 1887, 1c6–7]" correctly attributes this entry to June 3); *PR*, June 4, 1813, 3c2; Christie, *Memoirs of the Administration*, 85; NA (M148), Roll 11, January 2–June 30, 1813, item 110; July 1–December 30, 1813, item 42; Bixby, "Peter Sailly," 78–79, to quartermaster general. (Note: Everest, *War of 1812*, 109, quotes American casualties from British documents at the numbers shown here, noting that Rodney Macdonough "puts it somewhat less." It would appear that with Williams's corroborating information, Rodney Macdonough's figures are suspect.)

16. Bixby, "Peter Sailly," 78–79, to quartermaster general.

17. Everest, *War of 1812*, 111, 135; Hanson, *Lost Prince*, 238 (Note: *PR*, January 1, 1887, 1c8, incorrectly attributes this entry to June 10 instead of July 24), 239–40 .

18. NA (M148), Roll 12, July 1–December 30, 1813, item 21; Roll 11, July 1–December 30 1813, item 42; Tuttle, *Three Centuries*, 228.

19. Hanson, *Lost Prince*, 237–38, 240–41; *PR*, March 25, 1876, 1c4–5; Christie, *Memoirs of the Administration*, 87; Lewis, Benjamin Mooers to Colonel Smith, August 3, 1813; *PR*, March 25, 1876, 1c4–5; Bixby, "Peter Sailly," 80, to secretary of the treasury.

20. *PR*, January 1, 1887, 1c6–7; Bixby, "Peter Sailly 82, Ritter to Delord; Tuttle, *Three Centuries*, 240–41; NA (M148), Roll 12, July 1–December 30, 1813, item 66.

21. Clinton County Court Docket, 74; *PR*, July 9, 1813, 3c2: "On the 6th of August next, between the hours of 10 and 2, James Daugherty, for the murder of Ethan Bradley, is to be executed." The recording in the oyer and terminer court docket register incorrectly states that John Wait was the murdered party. Wait was a witness, as shown on the indictment papers among the records of Clinton County. Unfortunately, the name error became fixed after a mention in the first Peter Palmer article among the "Northern New York Historical Society Papers" of 1871,

published in the *Plattsburgh Republican*. The misidentification was further bolstered by its publication in a compilation called *Historical Sketch of Plattsburgh, NY*, printed in 1893 (p. 43). The error is carried forward, even today, by several contemporary web and print mentions. (Wait was probably amused at the reports of his death.)

22. Hanson, *Lost Prince*, 241.

23. BM, Hampton to Moores, Box 17, Folder 234; Box 8, Folders 114, 118; Hanson, *Lost Prince*, 241.

24. Hanson, *Lost Prince*, 241; *PR*, September 11, 1813, 3c2p; March 5, 1814, 1c1; October 16, 1813, 3c2.

25. *PR*, March 5, 1814, 1c2–3.

26. Ibid., October 9, 1813, 2c3; Hanson, *Lost Prince*, 241–46; *Connecticut* [Hartford] *Courant*, December 7, 1813.

27. Tuttle, *Three Centuries*, 386; Hanson, *Lost Prince*, 246.

28. Hanson, *Lost Prince*, 246–49.

29. Bixby, "Peter Sailly," 81, to secretary of the treasury; USN RG 45, secretary to captains, 149:163.

30. *PR*, January 1, 1814, 3c2.

CHAPTER 4

1. *PR*, January 1, 1814, 1c1–2; January 22, 1814, 3c3; January 8, 1814, 3c3; Hanson, *Lost Prince*, 248–49.

2. *PR*, January 8, 1814, 3c3; Hanson, *Lost Prince*, 248–50.

3. *PR*, January 22, 1814, 3c4; Hanson, *Lost Prince*, 250.

4. *PR*, March 12, 1814, 3c1–3.

5. Ibid., February 5, 1814, 3c4; War of 1812 Manuscripts, Benjamin Mooers to Charles D. Cooper, February 4, 1813 (Note: The Lilly Library has dated this letter as July 4, but Wilkinson's court-martial was held April 1814; he was not in command in July.); *PR*, February 19, 1814, 3c2; Macomb, *Order Book*, 1–3, 6–8; Hanson, *Lost Prince*, 251.

6. *PR*, February 12, 1814, 3c1; Macomb, *Order Book*, 8–10, 12; Hanson, *Lost Prince*, 251; *PR*, February 19, 1814, 3c2, p4c2.

7. *PR*, February 19, 1814, 3c4; Tuttle, *Three Centuries*, 52; Macomb, *Order Book*, 23; Hanson, *Three Centuries*, 251.

8. USN RG 45, secretary to captains, 149:223.

9. Tuttle, *Three Centuries*, 64; *PR*, March 12, 1814, 2c4; Hanson, *Lost Prince*, 251–52; Macomb, *Order Book*, March 6, 1814.

10. Crisman, *Eagle*, 18–19.

11. *PR*, March 19, 1814; Macomb, *Order Book*, 15, 72; Tuttle, *Three Centuries*, 82.

12. Tuttle, *Three Centuries*, 86, 89; *PR*, March 26, 1814, 2c4; April 9, 1814, 3c2; April 16, 1814, 2c1–2.

13. Tuttle, *Three Centuries*, 90–91; NAC, RG 8, Series I, 289; *PR*, April 23, 1814, 2c4, p3c1; Hanson, *Lost Prince*, 253.

14. Tuttle, *Three Centuries*, 98, 130; *PR*, April 9, 1814, 3c2; Macomb, *Order Book*, 13, 19, 27.

15. Macomb, *Order Book*, 13–14, 16, 19, 27; Hanson, *Lost Prince*, 253; *PR*, April 16, 1814, 2c3–4.

16. Tuttle, *Three Centuries*, 105; USN RG 45, Entry 147, pt. 2, no. 79; *PR*, June 14, 1814, 3c1 (from the *Middlebury Patriot*. Note: The actual *Saratoga*'s specifications were: 143 feet in length, 36½ feet abeam and, as armed by Macdonough, eight long twenty-four-pounders, six forty-two-pound carronades and twelve thirty-two-pound carronades [see Chapelle, *American Sailing Navy*, 298, 552].); *PR*, April 23, 1814, 3c1.

17. *PR*, April 23, 1814, 3c2; July 2, 1814, 2c3.

18. Macomb, *Order Book*, 21; *PR*, April 30, 1814, 3c4; May 14, 1814, 3c3.

19. *PR*, April 23, 1814, 2c4; July 2, 1814, 2c1; Macomb, *Order Book*, 32, 33; Hanson, *Lost Prince*, 253.

20. USN RG 45, Entry 147, pt. 2, no. 115; James Madison Papers, Library of Congress, Washington, D.C.

21. Macomb, *Order Book*, 39; *PR*, July 2, 1814, 1c2, 2c2–3 (*Courier*, London).

22. Macomb, *Order Book*, 48, 50, 62, 65; Hanson, *Lost Prince*, 253; *PR*, May 14, 1814, 3c3.

23. Macomb, *Order Book*, 40, 42; Christie, *Memoirs of the Administration*, 127; *PR*, May 14, 1814, 3c3–4; July 23, 1887, 1c4; Tuttle, *Three Centuries*, 132.

24. Tuttle, *Three Centuries*, 135–38; *PR*, June 4, 1814, 3c1; Christie, *Memoirs of the Administration*, 127.

25. Hanson, *Lost Prince*, 253–54.

26. *PR*, May 21, 1814, 3c1; USN RG 45, Entry 147, pt. 2, no. 134; *JRUSI*, 507; *PR*, June 4, 1814, 2c4; Bathurst to Ross (see Appendix II, first letter).

27. Hanson, *Lost Prince*, 254; *PR*, June 11, 1814, 3c1; July 2, 1814, 2c4; NAC, Bathurst to Prevost (see Appendix II, second letter]; Ells, *Calendar of Official Correspondence*, 317).

28. USN, RG 45, Letters Received by the Secretary, 1814, 6. (Note: Perry records the total as fifty-eight. The "List of Officers and Men Transferred to Lake Champlain" with the letter includes two sailing masters, three masters mates, one midshipman, one boatswain's mate, eleven able seamen, thirty-eight seaman and one boy, for a total of fifty-seven.); USN, RG 45, Entry 147, pt. 2, no. 143; USN, RG 45, letters received by the secretary, 1814, 21; Dobson, *Official Correspondence*, 49–51, Macdonough to secretary of the navy, enclosed w/ Izard letter to the secretary of war, June, 25, 1814; *PR*, June 18, 1814, 3c1.

29. *PR*, June 18, 1814, 3c1; Hanson, *Lost Prince*, 254–55.

30. *PR*, June 18, 1814, 3c1, p3c3 (*Albany Gazette*); Hanson, *Lost Prince*, 255.

31. *JRUSI*, 507.

32. USN RG 45, Entry 147, pt. 2, no. 146; Crisman, *Eagle*, 30; *PR*, June 25, 1814, 3c1.

33. NA M222, Roll 13, Nichols to Armstrong, June 23, 1814; *PR*, June 25, 1814, 3c1; Dobson, *Official Correspondence*, 35–37, Izard to Armstrong.

34. USN RG 45, Entry 147, pt. 2, no. 152; *PR*, September 9, 1849, 1c5.

35. Dobson, *Official Correspondence*, 56, Fisk to secretary of war; USN RG 45, Entry 147, pt. 2, no. 153.

36. *PR*, July 2, 1814, 3c1; NA M222, Roll 13, Nichols to Armstrong, June 23, 1814.

CHAPTER 5

1. Dobson, *Official Correspondence*, 51, secretary of war to Izard.

2. Ibid., 45–47, Izard to secretary of war; Altoff, *Amongst My Best Men*, 114; Greene, *Black Defenders*, 30, 34–38.

3. Hanson, *Lost Prince*, 255; Carter, Records of the Buffs (31), 516.

4. USN RG 45, Entry 441, pt. 2, no. 121; Entry 147, pt. 3, no. 4; Entry 147, pt. 2, no. 59; Crisman, *Eagle*, 43, 56, Appendix D. Note: Fitz-Enz, *Final Invasion*, 49, states that the Lake Champlain ships were "mostly constructed of unseasoned, soft pine planks seven inches thick."

5. *PR*, July 9, 1814, 3c3.

6. Hanson, *Lost Prince*, 255–56; NA M222, Roll 13, Nichols to Armstrong, July 19, 1814.

7. *PR*, July 30, 1814, 3c3; Crisman, *Eagle*, as in Macdonough-Boden Papers; *PR*, July 16, 1814, p2c3; USN RG 45, Entry 147, pt. 3, no. 7.

8. Hanson, *Lost Prince*, 256.

9. *PR*, July 30, 1814, 2c4; USN RG 45, Entry 147, pt. 3, no. 8; Hanson, *Lost Prince*, 257; Carter, Records of the Buffs (373), 516; (1203½:M78), 516; (1219:256), 516.

10. *PR*, July 30, 1814, 2c4; NA M222, Roll 13, Nichols to Armstrong, July 27, 1814.

11. Dobson, *Official Correspondence*, 57–59, Izard to secretary of war; McIntyre letter/map; NAC M24.

12. *PR*, August 6, 1814, 3c1; Bixby, "Peter Sailly," 83, to superintendent general of public supplies.

13. Hanson, *Lost Prince*, 257; *PR*, August 6, 1814, 3c1; Carter, Royal Hampshire Regiment, 166.

14. *JRUSI*, 507; Carter, Records of the Buffs (1707:109), 516; Graves, "Redcoats are Coming," 2; Hanson, *Lost Prince*, 257; Smyth, *Precis of the War*, 156–57.

15. USN RG 45, Entry 147, pt. 3, no. 12.

16. Carter, Historical Records of the Buffs, 420; Dobson, *Official Correspondence*, 65–67, Izard to secretary of war.

17. USN RG 45, Letters received by the secretary of the navy from captains, 1814, 6, 91.

18. Dobson, *Official Correspondence*, 71, Armstrong to Izard; Hanson, *Lost Prince*, 257–58.

19. *PR*, August 13, 1814, 2c4; *London Times*, October 11, 1814; Hanson, *Lost Prince*, 258; *JRUSI*, 508; Wood, *War with the United States*, 348, General Orders, Adjutant General's Office, August 16, 1814.

20. NA M222, Roll 13, Nichols to Armstrong, August 17, 1814; USN RG 45, Entry 147, pt. 3, nos. 18, 20; *PR*, August 27, 1814, 2c4.

21. Dobson, *Official Correspondence*, 71–72, Izard to secretary of war; Hanson, *Lost Prince*, 258.

22. USN RG 24, *Eagle* Log, August 21–27, 1814; *PR*, August 27, 1814, 3c1.

23. Dobson, *Official Correspondence*, 72–75, Izard to secretary of war.

24. Hanson, *Lost Prince*, 259–60; *London Times*, October 25, 1814.

25. Dobson, *Official Correspondence*, 143–44, Izard to Macomb.

26. Hanson, *Lost Prince*, 260–61; *Sentinel*, March 22, 1895, 1c5 (Reprinted from the *Lancaster Intelligencer*, March 9, 1895, a letter from General Alexander Macomb to his father residing in Lancaster: "Fort Morrau [*sic*], Sept 12, 1814."); USN RG 45, Entry 147, pt. 3, no. 25; *Eagle* Log, August 28; NA M222, Roll 13, Nichols to Armstrong, September 1, 1814.

27. Hanson, *Lost Prince*, 261; Christie, *Memoirs of the Administration*, 140; Champlain Society, 368, Pring to Yeo, September 12, 1814.

28. Hanson, *Lost Prince*, 261.

29. Ibid.; *JRUSI*, 509; *London Times*, October 21, 1814; *PR*, September 24, 1814, 1c3; Naval Historical Center, *Naval War of 1812*, vol. III, 223; Dobson, *Official Correspondence*, 75, Izard to secretary of war.

30. USN RG 24, *Eagle* Log, August 31; Barker, "Incident from the War," 66; *London Times*, October 21, 1814.

Chapter 6

1. *PR*, March 30, 1895, 1c3.

2. USN RG 45, Entry 125, Roll 39, no. 5; Hanson, *Lost Prince*, 261; USN RG 24, *Eagle* Log, September 1, 1814.

3. *JRUSI*, 509; *PR*, September 24, 1814, 1c3; Tuttle, *Three Centuries*, 278; USN RG 24, *Eagle* Log, September 2, 1814.

4. *JRUSI*, 509; *PR*, September 2, 1814, 2c3; Carter, Records of the Buffs (86:157), 518; Hanson, *Lost Prince*, 261; Clarke, *Boys Own Book*, 23–24; USN RG 45, letters received by the secretary of the navy from captains, Macdonough to Jones, September 3, 1814; USN RG 24, *Eagle* Log, September 3; Herkalo, *Journal of Averill*, 2, 8, 93.

5. Dobson, *Official Correspondence*, 144, O'Connor, assistant adjutant general, to Izard.

6. *JRUSI*, 509; Carter, Dorsetshire Regiment, vol. 1, First Brigade, Canada, 240–41; *JRUSI*, 509; Carter, Brisbane Papers, Baynes to Campbell, September 4, 1814; Champlain Society, 368, Pring to Yeo, September 12, 1814.

7. Hanson, *Lost Prince*, 261–63; *PR*, September 24, 1814, 1c3; Tuttle, *Three Centuries*, 281; Herkalo, *Journal of Averill*, 4; USN RG 24, *Eagle* Log, September 4, 1814; *JRUSI*, 509.

8. *PR*, March 30, 1895, 1c4; Macomb, *Order Book*, 69 [bracketed items] reported in the *PR*, September 24, 1814, 1c2 as follows: "since named Forts Brown & Scott"; *PR*, September 24, 1814, 1c3; Herkalo, *Journal of Averill*, 5–6; Hanson, *Lost Prince*, 261–63; USN RG 24, *Eagle* Log, September 5, 1814.

Note: Fitz-Enz, *Final Invasion*, 108 (citing North Country Notes, no. 103 [May 1974], an extract from the Bailey Collection, Burnt Hills, New York), refers to the mentioned rockets as being small "signaling" rockets, relying on the main text of the letter appearing in the Clinton County Historical Association's newsletter, *North Country Notes*. In reality, the rockets are known to have been larger battle-size devices; the complete letter, with its accompanying postscript regarding the weight of the rockets, is found among the Mooers documents at Plattsburgh State University.

Fitz-Enz devotes his Appendix G to rockets, stating that Congreve's field manual on the subject was published in 1804. Colonel Congreve, the man who perfected the weapon he developed in 1804, did indeed publish, but not until 1814, when the prince regent approved the formation of the "Rocket Corps." While one could petition the Museum at Woolwich for a copy of the publication, I found it easier to purchase the reprinted work from the Ottawa-based Museum Restoration Service a short distance from Plattsburgh.

9. Dobney, "Military Music"; Library of Congress, "Century of Lawmaking," 669; Macomb, *Order Book*, 65; *PR*, September 24, 1814, 2c4.

Note: Fitz-Enz, *Final Invasion*, 74 states, "There were no drummer boys, since the drums were now made out of heavy brass, rather than wood, and were man size." No evidence has been found that corroborates the British use of ordnance-issued brass drums at Plattsburgh. The British army historians state that the general size of the British side drum was made smaller between the years 1775 and 1800. The general size was reduced again when the brass shell was introduced for service; this happened "around the Waterloo period" (mid-1815). (British Army, "History of the Drum.) The British drummers at Plattsburgh would have carried wooden shell drums, as their American counterparts did. The British drums of the day were emblazoned with regimental colors, numbers, ordered ciphers (monograms) and perhaps battle honors or other devices; American drums were adorned with a patriotic eagle and regimental colors and numbers. (The Battle of Plattsburgh Association has a fine example of a militia "eagle drum" among its collections.) Britain's armies included drummer boys until the disastrous defeat of a British force by Zulu warriors in 1879 at Isandhlwana, South Africa. The deaths of the tortured young drummer boys in that action so affected the British public that the use of young musicians has not been allowed since.

10. Dobson, *Official Correspondence*, 82, to Major Bleeker, department quartermaster general, September 13, 1814; *JRUSI*, 509–10; *PR*, March 30, 1895, 1c4; Champlain Society, 397, Sinclair to Baynes, March 20, 1815; Carter, Historical Records of the Buffs, 420–21.

11. *PR*, September 24, 1814, 1c3; October 13, 1877, 1c3; Nelson, "Battle of Plattsburgh," 33–34; Bathurst to Ross, September 6, 1814, as in Adams, *History of the United States*, 312.

12. *PR*, September 24, 1814, 1c3; October 13, 1877, 1c3; October 17, 1894, 1c3; Carter, Historical Records of the Buffs, 420–21; Herkalo, *Journal of Averill*, 6–7.

13. *PR*, September 24, 1814, 1c3; *PR*, October 13, 1877, 1c3.

14. Brown, *Authentic History*, 216; *PR*, September 24, 1814, 1c3; March 30, 1895, 1c4; USN RG 24, *Eagle* Log, September 6, 1814; *PR*, November 20, 1841, 1c1–3; Carter, History of the Royal Sappers and Miners, 222; Champlain Society, 358, Macomb to secretary of war, September 15, 1814.

15. *JRUSI*, 509–10; *PR*, June 20, 1840, 3c2 ("En barbette," upon a raised area that enabled them to fire over the parapet and, thus, target a wider area; they were, however, open and more vulnerable than an embrasured gun (a gun stationed at an opening in the fortification.); NAC M24; Christie, *Memoirs of the Administration*, 141.

16. *PR*, September 24, 1814, 1c3–4; Champlain Society, 397, Sinclair to Baynes, March 20, 1815; Brown, *Authentic History*, 216; Carter, History of the Royal Sappers and Miners, 222; *PR*, September 24, 1814, 1c3–4; *JMSI*, 76–77, Macomb to General Jonathan Williams, September 18, 1814; Hanson, *Lost Prince*, 263–64.

17. USN RG 24, *Eagle* Log, September 6, 1814 ("Warp," to deploy a small anchor from a ship's boat and reel the ship by means of the capstan; i.e., without sail.); USN RG 24, *Eagle* Log, September 7, 1814; Hanson, *Lost Prince*, 263–64; Thomson, *Historical Sketches*, 320.

18. *PR*, March 30, 1895, 1c3; Herkalo, *Journal of Averill*, 7–8; Barker, "Incident from the War," 67; United States Army, Corps of Engineers, 381 ("Pioneers," troops detailed to clear obstructions placed in the line of march or before enemy fortifications, dig trenches and construct bridges and roads); *JRUSI*, 510; *PR*, September 24, 1814, 2c3.

19. *PR*, October 13, 1877, 1c3; September 24, 1814, 1c3; Richards, *Macomb Memoir*, 94; Berton, *Flames Across the Border*, 387.

20. Hanson, *Lost Prince*, 264; Herkalo, *Journal of Averill*, 8; USN RG 24, *Eagle* Log, September 8, 1814; *PR*, September 24, 1814, 1c3–4; Fitz-Enz, *Final Invasion*, 204 (refers to Vaughan as a member of the Vermont Militia. Vaughan was part of Mooers's New York militia. He does, however, properly identify Vaughan as New York Militia on page 123.); State of Vermont, 432; Vaughan, *Some Statements*; Everest, *Macomb*, 65; Richards, *Macomb Memoir*, 87, 92.

21. Carter, Records of the Buffs, 516–17; *PR*, March 30, 1895, 1c3; Christie, *Memoirs of the Administration*, 146.

22. Hanson, *Lost Prince*, 264–65; *JRUSI*, 510; Herkalo, *Journal of Averill*, 8.

23. Nelson, "Battle of Plattsburgh," 33–34; PRO, Weekly State of the Left Division. See also Herkalo, "British by the Numbers," 35–37. *PR*, September 24, 1814, 1c3–4; BM, Box 94, Gilliland to Mooers, September 9, 1814; *JMSI*, 76–77, Macomb to Williams, September 18, 1814.

24. Champlain Society, 381, Prevost to Downie, September 9, 1814; *JMSI*, 76–77, Macomb to Williams, September 18, 1814; *PR*, March 30, 1895, 1c3.

25. Hanson, *Lost Prince*, 265; Macomb, *Order Book*, 72; Everest, *Macomb*, 65; *PR*, September 4, 1880, 1c2–3; Macomb, Map, September 18, 1814; *PR*, March 30, 1895, 1c3; *JRUSI*, 510.

Note: Fitz-Enz's statement referring to the British use of smaller six- and ten-pound rockets at Plattsburgh (146–47) cannot be confirmed. The use of such small devices would have been of no consequence against the fortifications at Plattsburgh. William Congreve, the man after whom the rocket system was named, classifies the thirty-two-pounder as the standard bombardment rocket. The National Air and Space Museum notes that the thirty-two-pound rocket was the most widely used war rocket of the early nineteenth century; lacking further evidence, we might rightly assume that thirty-two-pound rockets were employed by Prevost's forces. The Congreve manufacturing process does not address a ten-pound rocket, as Fitz-Enz suggests; the closest is the nine-pounder. See Congreve, *Details of the Rocket System*, 53,56; NASM Congreve thirty-two-pounder rocket.

26. Hanson, *Lost Prince*, 265; BM, Box 8, Folder 114; USN RG 24, *Eagle* Log, September 10, 1814.

CHAPTER 7

1. USN RG 24, *Eagle* Log, September 11, 1814; *PR*, September 24, 1814, 1c3–4; *JRUSI*, 510–11 ("Scaling," the act of cleaning the inside of a ship's cannon by the explosion of a reduced quantity of powder [only]); Christie, *Memoirs of the Administration*, 144; *PR*, March 30, 1895, 1c4; Hitsman, *Incredible War*, 224; Champlain Society, 397, Sinclair to Baynes, March 20, 1815; Hanson, *Lost Prince*, 267; Fitz-Enz, *Final Invasion*, pictorial section, 119, 202, 258; *PR*, July 14, 1996, A-3, c4–6 ; West Point, class of 1812, class rank, 100; New York State Commission Plattsburgh Centenary, 36–37; NA RG 107, Macomb to secretary of war w/ map, September 18, 1814.

Note: Much has been made of late of the so-called Major DeRussy map presented by Fitz-Enz in the pictorial section of his offering and used as a supporting document in his 1995 claim that Pike's cantonment and the ford used by Prevost's army were located within the village. In his book, Fitz-Enz (who alternately spells the gentleman's name "Darusie") properly refers to DeRussy as a lieutenant, the man's rank in 1814. DeRussy was not granted the rank of major until 1824. While Fitz-Enz's pictorial legend states, "This map accompanied the official after-action report of the battle written by Brigadier General Alexander Macomb," the version reproduced is that of a tracing and did not appear until one hundred years later in the 1914 Centennial Commission's *The Battle of Plattsburgh: What Historians Say about It*. The original map, available from the National Archives, was drawn by Macomb; its compressed style does not represent the actual distances from the village to Power's western encampment and the cantonment's location. The map is Macomb's representation of the battle arena as he attempted to explain it. The DeRussy map is a tracing of the original map, and reliance on the use of this crude map has confused modern-day searchers in their attempt to locate relevant battle sites.

2. *PR*, November 17, 1883, 1c4; Clark, *List of Pensioners*, 57–59.

3. Fitz-Enz, *Final Invasion*, 141, 151. Note: The mention of the at-sea preservation technique for the metal appears to be influenced by Haythornthwaite, *Wellington's Military Machine*, 155. Reading from Fitz-Enz, one might assume that the guns of both fleets were made of bronze and that the British guns were "painted with a mixture of coal tar and saltwater to protect them from the corrosion of sea spray and foul weather." The lack of "sea spray" on Lake Champlain notwithstanding, in so far as I have been able to ascertain, the deck weapons of both fleets on September 11, 1814, were cast from iron. In describing these first minutes of the battle, Fitz- Enz (150, 151) repeats nearly word-for-word, without attribution, from Roosevelt, *Naval War of 1812*, 216, 217. Snider, *Glorious Shannon*, 312 (The flags of the *Confiance*, *Linnet* and *Chubb* are among the collections of the U.S. Naval Academy at Annapolis); Champlain Society, 397, Sinclair to Baynes, March 20, 1815; 368, Pring to Yeo, September 12, 1814; 373, Robinson to Pring, September 12, 1814; 438–42, court-martial testimony of Lieutenant Robertson; USN RG 45, Condition of Prize Vessels.

"Cat head," a horizontal timber extending from either side of the bow from which the main anchors are suspended. "Gig," a small rowboat for ferrying to and from the main ship.

4. *PR*, September 8, 1849, 1c5; Clark, *List of Pensioners*, 57–59.

5. Barker, "Incident from the War," 67 (see also note 7–19); *PR*, February 1, 1879, 1c2; United States Congress, Naval Affairs, 311–13; Clark, *List of Pensioners*, 57–59; USN RG 24, *Eagle* Log, September 11, 1814; USN RG 45, Condition of Prize Vessels.

Note: The claimed reproduction of the "heroic painting of the two major vessels, *Saratoga* and *Confiance*, locked in combat," presented by Fitz-Enz, *Final Invasion*, in his mid-book photo section (239–41) is actually a reproduction of the lower-left quadrant of the Thomas Birch painting *USS* Constitution *and HMS* Guerriere. The original Birch work hangs among the collection of the U.S. Naval Academy.

Fitz-Enz's three-page "Discussion of the Existence of a Shot Furnace on board *Confiance* is somehow moot in the presence of Nichol's forewarning and the capture inventory's matter-of-fact entry."

6. USN RG 45, letters from captains, Macdonough to Jones, September 14, 1814, 55. Fitz-Enz, *Final Invasion*, represents the Crab Island guns as sixteen-pound guns (121), while Richards, *Macomb Memoir*, says they were twelve-pounders (93). Fitz- Enz states that the rocky northern reef of the island is sand (159). Champlain Society, 442–46, Midshipman Thomas Eyre (court-martial testimony); 485, Carpenter Henry Cox (court-martial testimony), Defects of *Confiance* on September 11, 1814 (damage report); USN RG 45, condition of prize vessels; Champlain Society, Budd to Macdonough, September 13,

1814, 52; Fitz-Enz, *Final Invasion*, 159; Champlain Society, 429–32, Lieutenant Christopher Bell (court-martial testimony).

7. USN RG24, *Eagle* Log, September 11, 1814; *PR*, September 8, 1849, 1c5. In relating the detail of the *Confiance*'s last fighting moments, Fitz-Enz, *Final Invastion*, 161, states, "Most of the guns on the engaged side were dismounted and *Confiance*'s stout masts had been splintered, looking like bundles of matches strung together with knotted string. Her sails had been torn to rags." This statement comes mostly word-for-word from Roosevelt, *Naval War of 1812*, 217, without attribution.

8. Champlain Society, 373–77, Robertson to Pringle, September 12, 1814; NA T829, 147; Cooper, *History of the Navy*, 216; Fitch, Journals, 1056; *PR*, February 1, 1879, 1c5; Clark, *List of Pensioners*, 56; USN RG 45, condition of prize vessels; USN RG 45, letters from captains, Macdonough to Jones, 105.

9. Champlain Society, 397, Sinclair to Baynes, March 20, 1815 ("Merlon," solid part between two openings in a fortification wall.)

10. *JRUSI*, 510–12; Lucas, *Canadian War of 1812*, 206. A light five-and-a-half-inch howitzer was also reported to have accompanied this force (Champlain Society, 397, Sinclair to Baynes, March 20, 1815). In contrast to Robinson's description, Fitz-Enz, *Final Invasion*, 123, erroneously attributes the river's characteristics adjacent the "Maine Mill" as those of Pike's Ford: "The water slipped by in thin sheets over the solid rock bed." See also Mooers's description in chapter 2 of the river at Pike's ford being difficult to cross in the winter and summer and footnote 31 in chapter 2. *PR*, September 24, 1814, 1c3–4; Carter, Historical Record, 76th, 105–06; History of the Dorsetshire Regiment, vol. 1, First Brigade, Canada, 244:n.2; Fitz-Enz, *Final Invasion*, 165–67; Fitch, Journals, 1055; Richards, *Macomb Memoir*, 91.

11. *JRUSI*, 510–11; Fitz-Enz, *Final Invasion*, 167–68; *PR*, July 1, 1893, 1c3; Macomb, *Order Book*, 72–74; Brisbane Papers, Baynes to Brisbane, secret orders, September 12, 1814.

Note: Fitz-Enz quotes an uncited "letter home" in which Robinson is said to have written, "The advance was within shot, and full view of the Redoubt." I have found no discussion from Robinson or others that supports Fitz-Enz's statement: "Robinson, trailing Powers, crossed the Saranac and turned ninety degrees to the left with his brigade of thirty-four hundred." In contrast, Robinson's journal entry (above) indicates that the Twenty-seventh had not completely crossed the river when it was ordered to retreat.

In the same discussion, Fitz-Enz quotes an 1860 letter from John E. Wool to Lossing that expresses the opinion that Robinson's column

> *crossed the ford at Pike's Cantonment without resistance from the Militia, who retired as the column advanced, the head of which halted within a short distance of the rear of our works and remained there until the engagement of the two fleets was decided…The column in rear of the*

American works recrossed the Saranac without interruption, excepting the company in advance which not receiving the order to fall back and after waiting some time for the main column, went back to learn the cause of the delay, when they came in contact with General Strong's Vermont Militia, who killed and took prisoners the greater part of the company.

Wool's recollections were called into question when this and other claims were made public in the *Plattsburgh Republican*. Wool was, it seems, nowhere near Pike's ford; he was assigned by Macomb to Fort Moreau for the battle.

Curiously, Fitz-Enz states that the American militia "had no artillery to back their play," evidence of Lieutenant Sumpter's cannon notwithstanding.

12. Fitz-Enz, *Final Invasion*, 166; *PR*, September 24, 1814, 1c3–4, as in Hitsman, *Incredible War of 1812*, 77–78; Fitch, Journals, 1055; Brown, *Authentic History*, 217; *PR*, March 30, 1814, 1c4; Christie, *Memoirs of the Administration*, 144; Stanley, "Land Operations," 348.

13. USN RG 24, *Eagle* Log, September 11, 1814; Clark, *List of Pensioners*, 57–59, 61–62; USN RG 45, condition of prize vessels; *PR*, September 8, 1849, 1c5.

14. USN RG 24, *Eagle* Log, September 11, 1814; Clark, *List of Pensioners*, 57–59.

15. Hanson, *Lost Prince*, 267; Champlain Society, 397, Sinclair to Baynes, March 20, 1815; Baynes, *General Order Book*, September 13, 1814; USN RG 45, letters from captains, Macdonough to Jones, 105; Macomb, *Order Book*, 69–71; *London Times*, American Papers, November 25, 1814.

16. Hanson, *Lost Prince*, 267; *London Times*, October 20, 1814, 2cD; Macomb to Prevost, September 11, 1814; *PR*, March 30, 1895, as in Archives C, vol. 685, 196; USN RG 24, *Eagle* Log, September 12, 1814; Nelson, "Battle of Plattsburgh," 34.

17. *London Times*, October 29, 1814, 2cE; War of 1812 Manuscripts, officers of *Linnet* to Macdonough, September 15, 1814; United States Congress, Naval Affairs, 310; Champlain Society, 373, Robertson to Pring, September 12, 1814; USN RG 45, letters from captains, Macdonough to Jones, September 17, 1814, 62; Clark, *List of Pensioners*, 69–70; *London Times*, October 20, 1814, 2cD; *JMSI*, Macomb to Williams, September 18, 1814, 76–77; *PR*, March 30, 1895, 1c4; Carter, History of the Dorsetshire Regiment, 243–44; *PR*, June 26, 1909, 4c4–5.

18. *PR*, February 21, 1903, 1c4.

19. Ibid., 1c4–5; United States Congress, Naval Affairs, 311–13; NA (T829), "Supernumaries for Victuals."

Note: Macdonough's after-action report indicates Hale and Wood as "musicians"; the muster roll shows them as "privates" and does indicate their deaths on September 11. There was, apparently, one musician assigned for each of Macdonough's vessels. The four musicians from the Fifteenth and Thirty-third Regiments were George Mainwaring, Thomas Mellon, John

Goodrich and Israel Hooper; all survived. Beale's report (127) and Smith's recollection (109) are suspect.

20. *London Gazette*, November 19, 1814, 2337; Clark, *List of Pensioners*, 71–72.
21. *London Times*, November 28, 1814; Clark, *List of Pensioners*, 69–70.
22. NA T829, 147.
23. *PR*, September 24, 1814, 1c4, p2c1; *London Times*, October 29, 1814, p2cE; Macomb, *Order Book*, 72–74; Clark, *List of Pensioners*, 56–57.
24. War of 1812 Manuscripts, Henley to Macdonough, September 14–17, 1814. Regarding tensions between Macdonough and Henley, see Skaggs, *Thomas Macdonough*, 105, 142–44. War of 1812 Manuscripts, Henley to Macdonough, September 17, 1814; Macdonough to Winter (draft), October 8, 1814; USN RG 24, *Eagle* Log, September 18, 1814.
25. Clinton County Historical Society, no. 16, January 24, 1814.
26. USN RG 24, *Eagle* Log, September 14, 1814; Tuttle, *Three Centuries*, 299; War of 1812 Manuscripts, Macdonough to Thomas Gamble (draft), September 14, 1814.
27. Clark, *List of Pensioners*, 71–72; Hanson, *Lost Prince*, 267.
28. Carter, Records of the Buffs, 517; *London Gazette*, November 19–20, 1814 (verified against the transcript of the original as in Champlain Society, 354).
29. Carter, Records of the Buffs, 517; Northamptonshire Regiment, 184.
30. Bixby, Sailly to Quartermaster General Colonel Jenkins, September 17, 1814; Bixby, "Peter Sailly," 83; *PR*, September 1814, 2c2/3; Macomb, *Order Book*, 74–76, 95.
31. War of 1812 Manuscripts, letters to Macdonough, September 20, 1814; Tuttle, *Three Centuries*, 309–10; USN RG 24, *Eagle* Log, September 21, 1814.
32. Champlain Society, 364–66, Prevost to Bathurst, September 22, 1814.
33. USN RG 24, *Eagle* Log, September 24–29, 1814; *PR*, September 24, 1814, 2c4.

Chapter 8

1. Dobson, *Official Correspondence*, Izard to Monroe, 97–99.
2. United States Congress, Naval Affairs, Jones to Tait, October 3, 1814, 309; War of 1812 Manuscripts, Demarest (draft) to Macdonough, October 12, 1814; Macdonough to Bullus, October 12, 1814.
3. USN M125, Macdonough to Jones, October 15, 1814, 42, 126; *PR*, October 29, 1814, 2c3-4, p3c3; Bathurst to Pakenham, October 24, 1814 (see Appendix II, letter three); Lee, *Dictionary of National Biography*, 83–86.
4. Dobson, *Official Correspondence*, Sailly 86 to Macomb, October 26, 1814; 87, October 25, 1814; *United States House Journal*, November 14, 1814, 528; *PR*, October 29, 1814, 3c3.
5. Bathurst to Pakenham, October 24, 1814 (see Appendix II, letters four and five).
6. *London Times*, November 28, 1814, 3cD.

7. "Ordinary," the state of vessels that are laid up and out of commission (Smyth, *Sailors Lexicon*, 509); War of 1812 Manuscripts, Beale to Macdonough, December 21, 1814.

8. United States Congress, Naval Affairs, Beale, October 28, 1818, 172.

9. *PR*, December 24, 1814, 3c2–3.

10. *PR*, April 15, 1815, 3c2; United States Congress, Military Affairs, 41.

11. BM, Williams to Mooers, November 22, 1816, Box 17, Folder 234.

12. Kent-DeLord Collection. Henry DeLord, 66.7W 1/6, Leases 1803–48.

13. Lucas, *Canadian War of 1812*, 212; *JRUSI*, 519; Christie, *Memoirs of the Administration*, postscript. See also *Quarterly Review* (1822) and Cadell, *Some Account*.

14. Herkalo, *Journal of Averill*, 93; *PR*, July 8, 1826, 3c1. Fitz-Enz, *Final Invasion*, 111, incorrectly identifies the rifles as Springfield models with brass plaques.

15. *PR*, March 9, 1896, 1c3.

16. *Nile's Weekly Register*, vol. 3, September 1814–March 1815, 320.

Appendix II

1. Copy, UkENL, Alexander E.I. Cochrane Papers, MS 2343, Fols. 67–70. This letter was enclosed in Croker to Cochrane, May 21, 1814, Fol. 76. Bathurst addressed this letter to "Major General Edward Barnes or the Officer in command of the Troops detached from Gironde." General Barnes (1776–1838) was serving on the staff of the British army in the peninsula at this time. These orders actually went to Major General Robert Ross who was sent instead of Barnes to command the expeditionary force on the coast of the United States. "3 Regts. of Infantry with a proportion of Artillery from the Gironde—1do. [Regiment]—do. [of Infantry]—with one Company of do. [Artillery] from the Mediterranean—1 Battn. of Royal Marines with a proportion of Marine artillery." Note: As in the Naval Historical Center, *Naval War of 1812*, vol. 3, 72–74.

2. Much has been made of late regarding the plan in this "secret" letter by David Fitz-Enz, *Final Invasion*, who would have us believe that the document was "discovered" in London in 1922 but was somehow lost thereafter, becoming "one of the best-kept secrets in military history" until he (Fitz-Enz, xix) came across a copy of the "long-lost secret order" during a visit to Portugal. His posit, "Because its secret plan failed, the British government kept it confidential for over a century" (1–2) disregards even the basic documents relating to the war. While Fitz-Enz is correct in that the letter was, is and will remain one of the core primary documents regarding the conduct of the British campaign in the close of the war, it was by no stretch of the imagination unknown, "lost" or hidden. Fitz-Enz had only to consult any of the better-known contemporary works regarding Plattsburgh (Everest, *War of 1812*, 156; Hitsman, *Incredible War of 1812*, 214, 289–90;

Heinrich, "Battle of Plattsburgh," 41; or that in the nineteenth-century [1823] Cadell, *Some Account*, 136.)

3. National Archives, Kew Garden, War Office (WO) 6/2:26–29, as in *War of 1812* magazine.

4. Ibid.

5. Ibid.

Bibliography

Adams, Henry. *History of the United States of America during the Second Administration of James Madison*. Vol. 2. New York: Charles Scribner's Sons, 1921.

Altoff, Gerald T. *Amongst My Best Men: African-Americans and the War of 1812*. Put-in-Bay, OH: Perry Group, 1996.

The American Heritage Dictionary of the English Language. 3rd edition. Boston: Houghton Mifflin Company, 1992.

Ansley, Norman. *Vergennes, Vermont and the War of 1812*. Severna Park, MD: Brooke Keefer, 1999.

Auchinleck, Gilbert. *A History of the War between Great Britain & the United States of America during the Years 1812, 1813 & 1814*. Toronto, ON: Thomas Maclear, 1855.

Bailey-Moores Collection. Plattsburgh State University of New York, Feinberg Library Special Collections. Plattsburgh, New York.

Barker, A.S. "An Incident from the War of 1812." *Navy* (1914): 66–67.

"The Battle of Plattsburg." *Journal of the Military Service Institute* [*JMSI*] 12 (January 1891): 76–79.

Battle of Plattsburgh Commemoration Committee. Commemorative booklets. Plattsburgh, NY, various dates.

Baynes, Edward. *General Order Book*. Musee McCord Archives: M2664. Montreal, Quebec.

Beauchamp, William M. *Indian Names in New York*. Baldswinville, NY: William Beauchamp, 1893.

Beaumont Papers. William Beaumont, Writ. Yale University Medical Library. New Haven, Connecticut.

Beirne, Francis F. *The War of 1812*. New York: E.P. Dutton & Co., 1949.

Benn, Carl. *The Iroquois in the War of 181*. Toronto, ON: University of Toronto Press, 1998.

Berton, Pierre. *Flames Across the Border: 1813–1814*. Toronto, ON: McClelland & Stewart, 1981.

Bird, Harrison. *Navies in the Mountains*. New York: Oxford University Press, 1962.

Bixby, George S. "Peter Sailly (1754–1826): A Pioneer of the Champlain Valley, with Extracts from His Diary and Letters." *History Bulletin* 680 (1919).

Bloomfield, Joseph, and Zebulon Pike. *Letterbook, 1812–1813*. William L. Clements Library, University of Michigan. Ann Arbor, Michigan.

Brackcnridge, H.M. *History of the Late War between the United States and Great Britain*. Philadelphia: James Kay, Jun. & Bro., 1844.

Brannan, John, ed. *Official Letters of the Military and Naval Officers of the United States during the War with Great Britain in the Years 1812, 13, 14, & 15*. E351 B82. Plattsburgh State University of New York, Feinberg Library Special Collections. Plattsburgh, New York.

Brisbane Papers. William L. Clements Library, University of Michigan. Ann Arbor, Michigan.

Brown, Samuel R. *An Authentic History of the Second War for Independence*. Vol. 2. Auburn, NY: J.G. Hathaway, 1815.

Cadell, T. *Some Account of the Public Life of the Lieutenant-General Sir George Prevost, Bart. Particularly of his Services in the Canadas*. London: Strand and T. Egerton, 1823.

Carter, Roy, comp. *Roy Carter Papers*. Orpington, Kent: Roy Carter, 2005.
Dorsetshire Regiment. C.T. Atkinson, vol. 1.
The Dragon, April 1927. Records of the Buffs in Canada, 516–19.
Historical Record of the 76th Hindoostan Regiment History of the Northamptonshire Regiment, 1742–1934.
Historical Record of the Thirty-ninth, or the Dorsetshire Regiment of Foot.
Historical Records of the Buffs Royal Hampshire Regiment (vol. 1), 1st Battalion (Thirty-seventh Foot). C.T. Atkinson, 1950.
History of the Royal Sappers and Miners. Connolly, vol. 1.
Swiss in American Life. Zurich: Foundation Pro Helvetia, 1977.

The Champlain Society. *Select British Documents of the Canadian War of 1812*. Vol. 3. Edited by William Wood. Toronto, ON: The Champlain Society, 1926. Reprint, New York: Greenwood Press, 1968.

Chapelle, Howard I. *The History of the American Sailing Navy*. London: Salamander Books, Ltd., 1949.

Christie, Robert. *Memoirs of the Administration of the Colonial Government of Lower-Canada by Sir James Henry Craig, and Sir George Prevost from the Year 1807 until the Year 1815*. Quebec: Robert Christie, 1818.

Chronicles of Canada Series. Vol. 14, *A Chronicle of 1812*. Edited by George M. Wrong and H.H. Langton. Toronto, ON: Glasgow, Brooks & Co., 1920.

Clark, Byron N, ed. *A List of Pensioners of the War of 1812*. Burlington, VT: Clearfield, 1904. Reprint, Baltimore, MD: Genealogical Publishing Co., 1969.

Clarke, William. *The Boy's Own Book*. Boston: Munroe and Francis, 1829. Reprint, Bedford, MA: Applewood Books, 1996.

Clinton County Historical Society. "North Country Notes." Plattsburgh, New York.

Congreve, William. *Details of the Rocket System*. London: J. Whiting, 1814. Reprint, Ottawa, ON: Museum Restoration Service, 1970.

Cooper, J. Fenimore. *History of the Navy of the United States of America*. Vol. 1, 3rd edition. Cooperstown, NY: H&E Phinney, 1846.

County of Clinton, New York.

Maps, A73–77.

Oyer and Terminer Court Docket (1796–1824), vol. 2.

Oyer and Terminer Court Indictments, June 1813.

Crisman, Kevin J. *The Eagle*. Shelbourne, VT: New England Press, 1987.

———. *The History and Construction of the United States Schooner* Ticonderoga. Alexandria, VA: Eyrie Publications, 1982.

Denison, John L. *A Pictorial History of the New World*. New York: H. Bill, 1864.

"Documents, Artifacts, and Imagery." *War of 1812 Magazine* 16 (September 2011). http://www.napoleon-series.org/military/Warof1812/2011/Issue16/c_PakenhamOrders.html.

Dobney, Jayson Kerr. "Military Music in American and European Tradition." Timeline of Art History, Metropolitan Museum of Art. http://www.metmuseum.org/toah/hd/ammu/hd_ammu.htm.

Dobson, Thomas, comp. *Official Correspondence with the Department of War Relative to the Military Operations of the American Army under the Command of Major General Izard on the Northern Frontier of the United States in the Years 1814 and 1815*. Philadelphia: William Fry, 1816.

Duane, William. *A Military Dictionary*. Philadelphia, William Duane Publications, 1810.

Ells, Margaret, comp. *A Calendar of Official Correspondence and Legislative Papers of Nova Scotia, 1802–1815. Pub #3*. Halifax, NS: PANS, 1936.

Everest, Allan S. *The Military Career of Alexander Macomb and Alexander Macomb at Plattsburgh*. Plattsburgh, NY: Clinton County Historical Association, 1989.

———. *The War of 1812 in the Champlain Valley*. Syracuse, NY: Syracuse University Press, 1981.

"The Expedition to Plattsburgh, Upon Lake Champlain, Canada, 1814, with an account of it, from the Journal of the late General Sir Frederick Philipse Robinson, G.C.B." *Journal of the Royal United Service Institution [JRUSI]* 443 (August 1916): 499–522.

Fitch, Asa. Journals, 1809–79; 1847–78 (microfilm). New York Genealogical and Biographical Society. Bancroft Public Library. Salem, New York.

Fitz-Enz, David G. *The Final Invasion: Plattsburgh: The War of 1812's Most Decisive Battle*. New York: Cooper Square Press, 2001.

Forester, C.S. *The Age of Fighting Sail: The Story of the Naval War of 1812*. Edited by Lewis Gennett. Garden City, NY: Doubleday & Co., 1956.

Fredriksen, John C., comp. *War of 1812 Eyewitness Account*. Westport, CT: Greenwood, 1997.

Graves, Donald E. "The Redcoats are Coming!: British Troop Movements to North America in 1814." The War of 1812 Website. http://www.warof1812.ca/redcoats.htm.

———. *The Rocket's Red Glare*. Toronto, ON: Museum Restoration Service, 1989.

Greene, Robert E. *Black Defenders of America, 1775–1973*. Chicago: Johnson Publisher, Inc., 1974.

Hannay, James. *How Canada Was Held for the Empire*. London: T.C. and E.C. Jack, 1905.

Hanson, John H. *The Lost Prince: Facts Tending to Prove the Identity of Louis the Seventeenth, of France, and the Rev. Eleazar Williams, Missionary among the Indians of North America*. New York: G.P. Putnam & Co., 1854.

Hastings, Hugh, ed. *Public Papers of Daniel D. Tompkins, Governor of New York: 1807–1817*. Albany: State of New York, 1898.

Haythornthwaite, Philip J. *Wellington's Military Machine*. Kent, UK: Spellmount Limited, 1997.

Heinrichs, Waldo H., Jr. "The Battle of Plattsburg, 1814." American history honors diss. (Philip Washburn Prize), Harvard University, 1949.

———. "The Battle of Plattsburgh, 1814—The Losers." *American Neptune* 21, no. 1 (1961): 42–56.

Herkalo, Keith A. "British: By the Numbers." Battle of Plattsburgh Commemoration Program, 2005.

———. "The Location of Pike's Cantonment." *Antiquarian* 18 (2001): 1–6.

Herkalo, Keith A., ed. *The Journal of H.K. Averill, Sr.* Plattsburgh, NY: Battle of Plattsburgh Association, 2001.

Hitsman, J. Mackay. *The Incredible War of 1812: A Military History*. Edited by Donald E. Graves. Toronto, ON: Robin Brass Studio, 1999.

Hurd, D.H. *History of Clinton and Franklin Counties of New York*. Philadelphia: J.W. Lewis & Co., 1880.

Jay, William. "Table of the Killed and Wounded in the War of 1812." *Collections of the New York State Historical Society, Second Series* 3 (1849): 447–66.

Katcher, Philip. *Men-at-Arms, The American War 1812-14*. (Oxford: Osprey Publishing, 1990)

Kent-DeLord Collection. Plattsburgh State University of New York, Feinberg Library Special Collections. Plattsburgh, New York.

Lee, Sidney, ed. *Dictionary of National Biography*. Vol. 43. London: Smith, Elder & Co, 1895.

Lewis, Dennis M. "Plattsburgh's Veteran Exempts During the War of 1812." *Journal of the Company of Military Historians* 26, no. 1 (1984): 8–9

London Times

Lossing, Benson J. *Our Country: A Household History of the United States*. Vol. 2. New York: Johnson & Bailey, 1888.

———. *Pictorial Field-Book of the War of 1812*. New York: Harper & Bros., 1868.

Lossing, Benson J., ed. *Harper's Encyclopedia of United States History*. Vols. 6, 10. New York: Harper & Brothers, 1905.

Louisiana State University. "Statistical Summary America's Major Wars." Edited by Al Nofi, 2001. http://www.cwc.lsu.edu/cwc/other/stats/warcost.htm.

Lucas, C.P. *The Canadian War of 1812.* Oxford, UK: Clarendon Press, 1906.

Macdonough, Rodney. *The Life of Commodore Thomas Macdonough, U.S. Navy.* Boston: Fort Hill Press, 1909.

Macomb, Alexander. *A Concise System of Instructions and Regulations for the Militia and Volunteers of the United States.* Compiled by S. Cooper. Philadelphia: Frank Desilver, 1847.

―――. Map, September 18, 1814, NARA, RG 107. Records of the Office of the Secretary of War, Registered Letters, Main Series, 1801–89.

―――. *Military Order Book* (written at Plattsburgh, NY). St. Lawrence University, Owen D. Young Library Special Collections. Potsdam, New York.

Mahan, Alfred T. *Sea Power in Its Relations to the War of 1812.* Vols. 1, 2. Boston: Little, Brown, and Co, 1905.

Mahan, John K. *The War of 1812.* Gainesville, FL: DaCapo Press, 1972.

Mann, James. *Medical Sketches of the Campaigns of 1812, 13, 14.* Dedham, MA: H. Mann & Co., 1816.

Manucy, Albert. *Artillery Through the Ages: A Short Illustrated History of Cannon, Emphasizing Types used in America.* National Parks Service Interpretive Series, History No. 3. Washington, D.C: U.S. Government Printing Office, 1949, 1962.

McIntyre, Rufus. Letters, McIntyre to John Holmes, January 17, 1815, with map. NYS Library, Letters, 1813–15, Location system # (N) SC4150.

Muller, Charles G. *The Proudest Day.* New York: John Day Co., 1960.

Munday, John. *Naval Cannon.* Aylesbury, UK: Shire Publications Ltd., 1987.

Myer, Jesse S. *Life and Letters of Dr. William Beaumont* St. Louis, MO: C.V. Mosby Co., 1912.

National Aeronautic and Space Administration. NASM Space Artifacts: Rockets and Missiles, Congreve 32-pounder Rocket. http://www.nasm.si.edu/research/dsh/artifacts/RMCongreve32.htm.

National Archives of Canada
Public Record Office, CO 42, vol. 23. Bathurst to Prevost, June 3, 1814.
Public Record Office, CO. "Weekly State of the Left Division under the Command of Major General De Rottenburg, Head Quarters Plattsburg, September 8, 1814," RG 42:161.
RG 8, (MG 24), series I, vol. 682 M24, vol. F75-80, p. 18, F78. Report of Lieutenant John Lang, aide de camp, 19th Light Dragoons.

National Archives, Kew
Public Record Office, WO 6/2: 26-29.

National Archives Microfilm Publications, Washington, D.C.
(M125), Letters to the Secretary of the Navy from Captains, 1805–61, RG45.
(M148), Letters to the Secretary of the Navy from Officers Below the Rank of Commander, 1802–84, RG45.

(M221), Letters Received by the Secretary of War, Registered Series, 1801–60, RG107, Rolls 55–56, July 1812–May 1814; Roll 64, June 1814–December 1815.

(M222), Letters Received by the Secretary of War, Unregistered Series, 1801–60, RG107, 1814 I-M, Roll 12; N-R, Roll 13.

(M233), Register of Enlistments in the United States Army, 1797–1914, RG 94.

(M1856), Records of the Adjutant General's Office, Discharge Certificates and Miscellaneous Records Relating to the Discharge of Soldiers from the Regular Army, 1792–1815, RG94.

(T829), Miscellaneous Records, U.S. Navy, 1789–1925, RG 45.

    Muster Roll 1812–14, Lake Champlain Squadron, Roll 119.

    Muster Roll September 1814, Battle of Lake Champlain, Roll 141.

    1813–14 Stations, Lake Champlain & Whitehall, Roll 147.

British Naval MSS, Court-Martial, War of 1812 Lakes Champlain/Erie, Roll 412.

Naval Historical Center. *The Naval War of 1812: A Documentary History—1812*. Vol. 1. Edited by William S. Dudley. Washington, D.C: Naval Historical Center, 1985.

———. *The Naval War of 1812: A Documentary History—1813*. Vol. 2. Edited by William S. Dudley. Washington, D.C: Naval Historical Center, 1992.

———. *The Naval War of 1812: A Documentary History—1814*. Vol. 3. Edited by William S. Dudley. (Washington, D.C: Naval Historical Center, 2002.

Nelson, Gladys G., ed. "The Battle of Plattsburg." *University of Rochester Library Bulletin* 3, no. 2 (1948): 30–35.

New York State Library, Manuscripts and Special Collections, CQ161-222, Records 1809–17. U.S. Army Infantry Regiment 6th (Arranged by Company Commander's Name, Individual soldiers, DOB, Duty Activities, Wounds Received, Muster Rolls, Orders, Returns, Requisitions, Inspection Reports).

Nile's Weekly Register. Baltimore, MD: Franklin Press, 1812–15.

Nordhaus, William D. Table: "American Casualties from Major American Wars." http://www.nthposition.com/politics_nordhaus2.html.

Palmer, Peter S. *History of Lake Champlain: from Its First Exploration by the French in 1609 to the Close of the Year 1814*. 3rd edition. New York: Frank F Lovell & Co., 1886.

Peck, Taylor. *Round-Shot to Rocket*. Annapolis, MD: U.S. Naval Institute, 1949.

Perry, Kenneth A. *The Fitch Gazetteer: An Annotated Index to the Manuscript History of Washington County, New York*. Bowie, NY: Heritage Books, 1999.

Peterson, Charles J. *The Military Heroes of the War of 1812*. 10th edition. Philadelphia: Jason B. Smith & Co., 1858.

Peterson, Harold L. *Round Shot and Rammers*. Harrisburg, PA: Stackpole Books, 1969.

Phillips, E. Mary. *James Fenimore Cooper*. New York: John Lane Co., 1912.

Plattsburgh Centenary Commission. *The Battle of Plattsburgh: What Historians Say About It*. Albany, NY: J.B. Lyon, 1914.

Plattsburgh Republican

Plattsburgh Republican, comp. *Historical Sketch of Plattsburgh New York, From Its First Settlement to Jan. 1, 1893*. Plattsburgh, NY: Plattsburgh Republican, 1893.

Quarterly Review 28 (April/July 1822).

Richards, George H. *Memoir of Alexander Macomb: The Major General Commanding the Army of the United States*. New York: M'Elrath, Bangs & Co., 1833.

Roosevelt, Theodore. *The Naval War of 1812*. 3rd edition. Edited by Caleb Carr. New York: Modern Library, 1999.

Sentinel [Plattsburg, New York]

Severance, Frank H. *Notes on the Literature of the War of 1812*. Toronto, ON: Ontario Historical Society, 1912. http://historical.library.cornell.edu/gifcache/nys/nys393.

Skaggs, David C. *Thomas Macdonough: Master of Command in the Early U.S. Navy*. Annapolis, MD: Naval Institute Press, 2003.

Skeen, C. Edward. *Citizen Soldiers in the War of 1812*. Lexington: University Press of Kentucky, 1999.

Skinner, St. John B.L. *The Battle of Plattsburgh: An Address Delivered before the Plattsburgh Lyceum, Feb. 18, 1835*. Plattsburgh, NY: Plattsburgh Lyceum, 1835.

Smyth, Major General Sir James Carmichael. *Precis of the Wars in Canada from 1755 to the Treaty of Ghent in 1814*. London: C. Roworth, 1826.

Smyth, W.H. *Chapman the Sailor's Lexicon*. New York: Hearst Books, 2005.

Snider, C.H.J. *The Glorious "Shannon's" Old Blue Duster and Other Faded Flags of Fadeless Fame*. Toronto, ON: McClelland & Stewart, 1923.

Stanley, George F.G. "The War of 1812 Land Operations." *Canadian War Museum Historical Publication* 18 (1983).

State of Vermont. *Report of Roster of Soldiers in the War of 1812*. Compiled by Herbert T. Johnson. Colchester: State of Vermont, 1933.

————.*Roster of Vermonters Who Served in the War of 1812*. Compiled by Martha T. Rainville. Colchester: State of Vermont, 1998.

Stellwagen, Daniel S. Papers of Daniel S. Stellwagen, 1814–1827. Library of Congress, Archival Manuscript Material Collection, mm70048751.

Thomson, John Lewis. *Historical Sketches of the Late War between the United States and Great Britain*. 5th edition. Philadelphia: Thomas Desilver, 1818.

Tomes, Robert. *Battles of America by Sea and Land*. Vol. 3. New York: Virtue & Co., 1861.

Town of Plattsburgh, New York. Roads and Bridges, 1798–1884.

Tritton, Roger, ed. *The Visual Dictionary of Ships and Sailing*. New York: Doring Kindersley, 1991.

Tuttle, Mrs. George F., ed. *Three Centuries in Champlain Valley*. *Tercentenary*. Plattsburgh, NY: Saranac Chapter, DAR, 1909.

United Kingdom, British Army. "The History of the Drum." http://www.army.mod.uk/linkedfiles/asc/History_of_the_drum.pdf.

United States Air Force. *National Register Evaluation of Archaeological Sites* [at] *Plattsburgh Air Force Base*. Brooks AFB, TX: Air Force Center for Environmental Excellence, 1998.

United States Army. *Military Academy Class of 1812, Class Rank*. West Point, NY, 1812.

United States Army Corps of Engineers. *Engineers of Independence: A Documentary History of American Engineers in the American Revolution, 1775–1783*. Engineering Pamphlet 870-1-6, glossary. http://www.usace.army.mil/inet/usace-docs/engppamphlets/ep870-1-6/glossary.pdf.

United States Congress. *American State Papers, Naval Affairs*. Vol. 1, *Naval Affairs*; Vol. 2, *Military Affairs*. Washington, D.C: Gales and Seaton, 1834.

United States House. *Journal of the U.S. House of Representatives*. 1814.

United States Library of Congress. "Damages for Enlisting a Minor." *A Century of Lawmaking for a New Nation: U.S. Congressional Documents and Debates, 1774–1875*. http://memory.loc.gov.

United States Navy

RG 11. General Records of the U.S. Government.

RG 24. Navy Deck Logs, USS Surprise (Eagle) 8-21-1814 to 9-29-1814. [The only deck log of any of the major ships known to exist; penned by Daniel Records acting sailing master. See Stellwagen for gunboat material.]

RG 45. Subject File, Box 742, Lake Champlain, 110, Condition of Prize Vessels, November 21, 1814.

RG 45. Area File 7, 1812.

RG 45. Secretary of the Navy to Captains, Roll 11, pt. 2 (as in Eagle).

RG 45. Entry 147, Roll 5, pt. 2, 3 (as in Eagle).

RG 45. Entry 441. Secretary of the Navy to Agents, Roll 1, pt. 2.

RG 45. Entry 125. Letters Received by the Secretary of the Navy from Captains (as in Eagle).

U.S. Census, Clinton County, NY. Washington, D.C.: United States Government, 1810.

Vaughan, Nathan A. *Some Statements as to the Ancestry of the Vaughan Family as Well as Some of Their Descendents*. San Francisco, CA, 1904.

von Steuben, Frederick William. *Regulations for the Order and Discipline of the Troops of the United States*. Boston: I. Thomas and E.T. Andrews, 1794. Reprint, Mineola, NY: Dover Publications, Inc., 1985.

Wallcut, R.F. *The Loyalty and Devotion of Colored Americans in the Revolution and the War of 1812*. Boston: University of British Columbia, 1861.

War of 1812 Manuscripts and Special Collections. Indiana University Lilly Library. Bloomington, Indiana.

Warren Letters [WAR53]. Sir John Borlase Warren. National Maritime Museum. Greenwich, England.

Whitehill, Walter M. "Cooper as a Naval Historian—A Reappraisal." *New York History* 35, no. 4 (1954): 468–79.

Wood, William. *The War with the United States*. Toronto, ON: Glasgow, Brook & Co., 1920.

Index

About the Author

K eith Herkalo was born in Plattsburgh, New York, in 1948 and raised in Philadelphia and Plattsburgh (the family summered in Plattsburgh every year). After more than a decade in the military and an additional decade working for military equipment development firms in the Washington, D.C. area, he returned with his family to Plattsburgh (the proverbial return to Woebegon). It was then that he became more interested in Plattsburgh's history and specifically Plattsburgh's involvement in the War of 1812.

He is an amateur historian who is the research catalyst behind the archaeological rediscovery of the 1812 camp known as Pike's Cantonment, the editor of *The Journal of H.K. Averill, Sr.: An account of the Battle of Plattsburgh and Early North Country Community*, has authored numerous local history articles and has been a frequent speaker in local history venues for many years.

He is the city clerk of Plattsburgh; a founding member and current president of the Battle of Plattsburgh Association; a musician, theater buff, boat builder, sailor, diver, woodworker, plaster restorer and an 1812-era reenactor.

With his wife, Dr. Joy Demarse, Keith is currently building their energy-efficient, solar-powered retirement home.